The Capability Approach in Practice

This important book maps much of the work operationalising the capability approach to date, and shows one of the ways in which that approach can be used for global development agenda setting. Given the significance of the Post-SDG agenda, and the importance of both local and global knowledges, this book makes an important contribution to these areas. Anyone interested in mainstream development ethics, goal setting, and the capability approach will find this book an excellent resource.

—Krushil Watene, Massey University, New Zealand

In this lucid and systematic study, Morten Fibieger Byskov provides challenging answers to three questions at the core of both development ethics and the capability approach to development: (1) Which should be the goals of development and a "development agenda?" (2) Who should decide? and (3) What methods should be employed in deciding? The "inclusive framework" for which Byskov argues achieves a nice balance between normative and empirical aspects of development and between the rights of local stakeholders and contributions of a variety of experts. This engaging volume will be a "must read" for development ethicists, capability theorists, and development practitioners.

—David A. Crocker, University of Maryland, United States

This book develops a philosophical framework for selecting goals for development purposes. This inclusive and democratic framework integrates a variety of resources including philosophical theory, empirical analysis, stakeholder deliberations, local knowledge, and advice from development experts. The author contends that we must provide good reasons and arguments in order to justify a particular development agenda. That is, we need to ask *why* we choose certain kinds of development goals over others, *why* we include certain agents in the selection process and not others, and *why* we select goals through one method rather than another.

In response to these questions, the author argues that development should aim at expanding people's capabilities and functionings. Capabilities and functionings—capabilities that have been realized—tell us what people are actually able to do and be with their resources, goods, and formal freedoms. He advances the view that local stakeholders should have more authority in deciding what a development agenda looks like. This *claim to local authority in development* can be interpreted both as a claim to political authority and expert authority. Finally, the author argues that ad hoc, foundational, procedural, and mixed (multi-stage) methods need to be synthesized in order to select the best capabilities and functionings for development.

The Capability Approach in Practice provides a philosophical and systematic approach to setting development agendas. It is an important contribution to the literature on the capability approach and development ethics, which will appeal to a broad range of scholars within philosophy and development studies.

Morten Fibieger Byskov is a postdoctoral researcher at the Interdisciplinary Ethics Research Group, Department of Politics and International Studies, University of Warwick, UK.

Routledge Research in Applied Ethics

Vulnerability, Autonomy and Applied Ethics
Edited by Christine Straehle

Refugees and the Ethics of Forced Displacement
Serena Parekh

Procreation, Parenthood, and Educational Rights
Ethical and Philosophical Issues
Edited by Jaime Ahlberg and Michael Chobli

The Ethics of Climate Engineering
Solar Radiation Management and Non-Ideal Justice
Toby Svoboda

Corporal Punishment
A Philosophical Assessment
Patrick Lenta

Hobbesian Applied Ethics and Public Policy
Edited by Shane D. Courtland

Does the Pro-Life Worldview Make Sense?
Abortion, Hell, and Violence Against Abortion Doctors
Stephen Kershnar

The Injustice of Punishment
Bruce N. Waller

Friendship, Robots, and Social Media
False Friends and Second Selves
Alexis M. Elder

The Capability Approach in Practice
A New Ethics for Setting Development Agendas
Morten Fibieger Byskov

The Capability Approach in Practice

A New Ethics for Setting Development Agendas

Morten Fibieger Byskov

Routledge
Taylor & Francis Group
LONDON AND NEW YORK

First published 2018 by Routledge

2 Park Square, Milton Park, Abingdon, Oxon, OX14 4RN
605 Third Avenue, New York, NY 10017

Routledge is an imprint of the Taylor & Francis Group, an informa business

First issued in paperback 2020

Library of Congress Cataloging-in-Publication Data
A catalog record for this book has been requested

ISBN: 978-1-138-58445-7 (hbk)
ISBN: 978-0-367-73466-4 (pbk)

Typeset in Sabon
by Apex CoVantage, LLC

Contents

Tables

Abbreviations and Acronyms

cf.	(L.) *conferre* = see; as referred to
e.g.	(L.) *exempli gratia* = for example
et al.	(L.) *et alii* = and other authors
GDP	gross domestic product
HDI	Human Development Index
HDR	Human Development Report(s)
ICSU	International Council for Science
ICT	information and communication technology
IDTs	International Development Targets
i.e.	(L.) *id est* = that is; meaning
IPCC	Intergovernmental Panel on Climate Change
IPEC	International Programme on the Elimination of Child Labour
ISSC	International Social Science Council
MDGs	Millennium Development Goals
NGO	nongovernmental organization
OECD	Organisation for Economic Co-operation and Development
OWG	Open Working Group
Rio+20	United Nations Conference on Sustainable Development 2012
SDGs	Sustainable Development Goals
UN	United Nations
UNDP	United Nations Development Programme
UNESCO	United Nations Educational, Scientific and Cultural Organization
WHO	World Health Organization

Acknowledgments

There are countless people who have shaped my thinking about the topics of this book and to whom I owe my deepest gratitude, no one more so than Ingrid Robeyns. I am deeply indebted to Ingrid for taking me on as her PhD student and I have grown as an academic and as a person under her guidance. I have benefitted immensely from Ingrid's inquisitive personality, our many discussions on the foundation of the capability approach, and her always on-point, in-depth comments, corrections, and challenges to earlier drafts of this book. I am also grateful for the guidance of Bert van den Brink whose positive attitude was a motivating factor through the intense period of writing, and his expertise and insights have made this a much better book.

During the writing of this book I have encountered many inspiring colleagues, many of whom I am lucky to have come to consider among my friends. Especially my involvement with the Human Development and Capability Association (HDCA) and the International Development Ethics Association (IDEA) has been an important source of inspiration and fruitful discussion on the themes of this book. I am especially indebted to Sine Bagatur, Constanze Binder, Rutger Claassen, Flavio Comim, Andrew Crabtree, David A. Crocker, Julian Culp, Willem van der Deijl, Jay Drydyk, Oscar Garza, Des Gasper, Pablo Gilabert, Rebecca Gutwald, Conrad Heilman, Lori Keleher, Serene Khader, Stacy J. Kosko, Sem de Maagt, Eric Palmer, Joe Philips, Mozaffar Qizilbash, Henry Richardson, Marco Sebastianelli, Mitu Sengupta, Elaine Unterhalter, Toon Vandevelde, Sridhar Venkatapuram, Jack Vromen, Krushil Watene, and Thomas Wells.

A shortened version of Chapter 4 has been published in volume 45, number 3, of *Oxford Development Studies* with the title "Third Wave Development Expertise." I am thankful to Frances Stewart and two anonymous reviewers for their comments and revisions to this paper. A shortened version of Chapter 6, titled "Methods for the Selection of Capabilities and Functionings," has been accepted for inclusion in the book *New Frontiers of the Capability Approach*, edited by Flavio Comim, Shailaja Fennel, and P. B. Anand, to be published by Cambridge

University Press. I am indebted to Flavio Comim for his extensive comments and revisions to this chapter.

At Routledge I have benefitted from the editorial advice and assistance of Andrew Weckenmann, whose suggestion for a new title I have enthusiastically adopted; and Alexandra Simmons, whose patience with my many questions has been much appreciated. I would also like to thank two anonymous reviewers for their comments and suggestions for improvements to the manuscript.

Lastly, the work on this book was made a lot easier by the continued support and encouragement from my dearest friends and family: Ida, Ruth and Knud, Jeppe, Katja and Peter, Sune, Nille, and Jon. Knowing that my friends and family would always be there for me has been an invaluable part of this process.

1 The Importance of Development Agendas

What do we mean when we talk about *development*? Admittedly, this is an equivocal and ambiguous question at best. Alkire and Deneulin (2009, 1), for example, highlight some of the many meanings of 'development':

> For some, development means more material prosperity: owning money, land, and a house. For others, development concerns liberation from oppression. Some see development as a new word for neo-colonialism, and despise it. For still others, development is a holistic project of personal, social and spiritual progress. In many contexts we speak of the "development" of a child or the "development" of new software as if development completes something as yet unfinished.

This book is not about the psychosocial development of children or about software development. Rather, the sense of development I am concerned with here are the personal, social, environmental, economic, and institutional circumstances that make up human life and that can be the subject of academic and political discussions as well as of public policy-making. Yet even in this narrowed-down sense of development there are as many approaches to development as there are ethical theories, each with their own view on what successful development is. Successful development could be equated with economic growth, for example, or be achieved through green technologies and sustainable living. For others, development concerns merely extreme cases of deprivations and should primarily aim to secure that people (especially in developing countries, war zones, and catastrophe areas) have adequate conditions for survival.

One particular aspect of development is the selection, definition, and formulation of the goals that development should achieve. In this book, I shall follow the example of the United Nations (UN) and refer to the set of goals, aims, and targets that development should achieve (or at the very least pursue) as a *development agenda*. Accordingly, a development agenda, as I shall define it here, is a normative convention, agreement, decree, or aspiration that specifies a set of goals that should be achieved by international, national, and local development efforts, such as concrete development interventions and projects, as well as national public policies.

Since their adoption in 2000, the global development agenda has primarily been driven by the UN's Millennium Development Goals (MDGs; Vandemoortele 2012; Fukuda-Parr 2012, 2–4). The MDGs aimed to set out concrete goals and targets representing the commitments made in the Millennium Declaration (United Nations 2000), which includes the eradication of extreme poverty, gender equality, and global education (United Nations 2015b). Although much progress has been made, the extent to which the development community has achieved the MDGs is less clear and often depends on how the data are interpreted (Vandemoortele 2012; Fukuda-Parr 2012, 9). The end of 2015 was the self-imposed deadline for achieving the MDGs. Recent years have thus seen a fierce debate about how to advance toward a post-2015 development agenda. Within the UN system, this debate has resulted in the proposal for and adoption of a new set of goals, the Sustainable Development Goals (SDGs), which promise to address the shortcomings of the MDGs.

In this book, I start from the discussions on a post-2015 development agenda and consider what is at stake when selecting the relevant goals for a development agenda in general and in relation to a post-2015 agenda in particular. I propose to take a step back to consider three fundamental questions that relate to the task of selecting development goals. First, what *kinds* of goals should a development agenda adopt? Second, *who* should decide what goals are included on the development agenda? And third, *how* should we select and specify these goals? In asking and answering these questions, the book contributes to the literature by setting out a comprehensive and inclusive framework for selecting development goals in general and for a development agenda in particular.

By answering these three questions I set out what I call an integrative framework for setting development agendas. Now, we may of course ask whether the more important task of development is to set out a justifiable development agenda or, rather, to *do* development. While these two aspects of development ideally go in tandem, there is something to be said for the latter view: we cannot always wait around for a justifiable agenda, which may never come, in order to act. However, there are good reasons to first engage in discussions on a development agenda before we start implementing rash development initiatives. Having a justifiable development agenda on hand ensures that development efforts are coordinated and targeted rather than disparate and possibly damaging.

Why is it important that we set out such an integrative framework for setting development agendas? What is the significance of the inquiries that I will be making in this book? Why is it important to consider what will be on a development agenda, who will decide this, and how they will do so? As alluded to by Alkire and Deneulin, development efforts have been quite fragmented and incoherent. Development agendas are shaped by normative beliefs (Cooke 2004), technocratic assumptions (Chambers 1997; Ferguson 1990, 1994), and/or political interests (Easterly 2013). Throughout this book, we will see how such different approaches to development, representing distinct normative assumptions and political interests, directly or indirectly determine how a development agenda is set and what it eventually looks like.

It is imperative that we can provide good reasons and arguments for our answers to these three questions in order to justify the consequent development agenda. That is, we need to ask *why* we choose certain kinds of development goals over others, *why* we include certain agents in the selection process and not others, and *why* we select goals through one method rather than another. In other words, my inquiries in this book are important because they help us to determine why we demand that development efforts should achieve a certain set of goals: why do we consider this agenda a better or more justifiable guideline for development than any other?

This is the task I face in this book. To anticipate, the framework I develop in this book holds that the goals of a development agenda (a) should be conceptualized in terms of capabilities and functionings, (b) cannot arbitrarily ignore the values and preferences of the people to whom they apply, and (c) should be selected as a product of a procedure of mediated deliberation between local agents and external development experts. In the following two sections, I briefly consider the importance of each of the three fundamental questions before I provide a chapter overview, which summarizes the elements of the framework for the selection of development goals that will be developed throughout this book.

1.1 Three Fundamental Questions of Setting a Development Agenda

Before we can begin to consider what a development agenda should look like—what concrete goals it should include—we need to answer three fundamental questions. The three fundamental questions are, first, what *kinds* of goals a development agenda should include; second, *who* should be involved in setting a development agenda; and, third, *how* they should go about doing so. Before I summarize the framework that I set out to answer these three questions, let me briefly consider each question in order to bring out their importance and, hence, why they need to be adequately addressed.

The first question, which is the subject of Chapter 2, concerns what kinds of goals a development agenda should include. Development goals come in many shapes and sizes. For some, development should aim to provide local stakeholders with basic means and resources for human survival, such as housing, food, clean water, security, medicine, and so on. For others, development goals should reflect the most efficient investments or the initiatives that have the most positive impact on people's lives. Yet others see development as a means to economic improvement and growth, while some hold that development goals should aim to secure socioeconomic opportunity and/or equality.

What is important to note is that our normative view of development—basic needs, economic growth, and so on—is to a large extent constitutive of a development agenda and its goals, which in turn influence concrete development initiatives, efforts, and policies. An agenda focused on basic means for human survival would not consider equal opportunity in the job market, for example, as normatively relevant, while an efficiency-focused agenda—the strategy taken up by the Gates Foundation[1]—would attribute more normative weight to those goals that could give us the most return for our investment. To wit, the *kinds* of goals that our agenda should reflect influence the *specific* goals that the agenda includes and excludes.

The second question that I shall attempt to answer in this book asks who should be involved in the setting of a development agenda. This question is addressed in Chapters 3 and 4 in particular. Development involves many different stakeholders, ranging from international organizations and donor countries to national governments, NGOs, and development practitioners and the local citizens and interest groups who will ultimately be affected by the implementation of a development agenda. Each of these (groups of) stakeholders will want to have a say in the design of a development agenda. It thus becomes important to determine who has a rightful claim to take part in this process.

While the task of setting a development agenda has traditionally belonged to aid donors—those financing the development efforts—and so-called development experts, a claim that local stakeholders should be granted more authority in this regard has emerged within the development literature in recent years. The second question thus concerns on what basis local stakeholders can claim authority in the context of setting a development agenda.

As I will be using the term frequently throughout, it is important here to note that in this book I define 'local stakeholders' quite broadly and unspecific. Primarily the term denotes the intended beneficiaries of a development agenda. Who the intended beneficiaries are depends on the context and is something that should be specified in the process of setting out the particular agenda, as I will argue as part of the second question. Thus, as is often the case in development contexts, 'local stakeholders' may refer to specific indigenous peoples, socioeconomically disadvantaged communities (including in more affluent countries), inhabitants of regions exposed to (natural) risks, hazards, and conflicts, as well as, more broadly, to people in the Global South.

The third and final question that I address in this book concerns by which method we should select the goals of a development agenda. This methodological investigation will be the subject of Chapters 5 and 6. There are several different methods for the selection of development goals: we may want to base the goals on normative theory—such as a theory of justice or a human rights theory—or maybe we would like the goals to represent the subjective preferences, values, and norms of local stakeholders; we may want our method to be based on quantitative statistics or we may take a more qualitative approach.

Again, the question of the right methodology is fundamental because the method by which we select development goals has the potential to influence the specific goals of the agenda. A method based on a theory of justice, for example, would likely arrive at a list of goals that represent basic principles of justice, while a more empirically oriented method would arguably identify development goals that reflect real-life, nonideal circumstances and needs.

How we answer these three fundamental questions may crucially influence the particular list of development goals that a development agenda contains, and how we justify a particular development agenda thus to a great extent relies on how we justify the answers to the three fundamental questions. In this book, I develop and argue in support of my own framework for the setting of a development agenda, which provides answers to the three questions asked. In the following section, I provide a short overview of the framework that I will develop and defend and how it addresses the three fundamental questions.

1.2 An Inclusive Framework for the Setting of a Development Agenda

What does the framework that I set out in this book look like? How does it address the three questions I set out in the previous section? The framework that is developed in this book aims to provide an approach to setting development agendas that can integrate different sources of insight and knowledge that is relevant for development. In particular, I defend the view that local stakeholders should have a larger say in what a development agenda looks like. In this way, the framework will integrate sources such as philosophical theory, empirical analysis, stakeholder deliberations, and advice from development experts. For this reason, I label the view that I present in this book *an inclusive framework for setting development agendas.*

As I argued in the previous section, setting out a justifiable development agenda requires us to consider four fundamental questions. In the following, I shortly consider each question and how they will be addressed in the four main chapters of this book.

The first question I consider in this book concerns what kinds of goals we should pursue as a matter of development. Are we aiming for economic development? Do we primarily concern ourselves with the development of public institutions and social security? Is development a tool to combat structures of oppression? In Chapter 2, I argue that my framework, in order to answer the first question, would benefit from adopting the idea of *human development*. Human development has its origins in two academic developments in the 1970s, namely the emergence of the field of development ethics, pioneered by Denis Goulet (1971), and Amartya Sen's (1979, 1989) capability approach. Development ethics and the capability approach both introduced a concern for human beings to the field of (economic) development. How, they asked, can we achieve development that is ethically sound or morally justified?

The capability approach especially provides an answer to this question. Rather than merely providing people with a set of resources or the basic conditions for human survival, its proponents have argued, development should aim at expanding people's capabilities and functionings. Capabilities are defined as the real freedom that people have to do or be certain things. Functionings are capabilities that have been realized. The benefit of focusing on capabilities and functionings is that it tells us what people are *actually* able to do and be with their resources, goods, and formal freedoms. We are thus concerned with the ends of development rather than the means.

A focus on the means to development, to the contrary, ignores the fact that people are involuntarily subject to various factors that influence the extent to which they are able to successfully convert resources into actual opportunities or realized doings and beings. For example, a person in a wheelchair would arguably be able to do less with the same amount of economic resources than an able-bodied person. Even though they would be equally well-off in terms of means, such as economic resources, the person in the wheelchair is worse off in terms of what she can do or be with those resources simply due to the fact that she has more necessary expenses for her wheelchair, medicine, and physical therapy. In other words, in order to assess the extent to which people are well off we need to focus on what they are able to do or be with a set of resources rather than on the amount of resources they have.

For these reasons, in this book I shall be arguing that the first element of an inclusive framework for selecting development goals should be the conceptualization of development goals in terms of capabilities and functionings—what people are able to do and be—rather than in terms of the resources, goods, and formal freedoms they possess or have access to.

The concepts of human development, capabilities, and functionings do not specify what goals are relevant for development, however. As

Robeyns (2011) argues, the concept of capabilities and functionings is morally neutral:

> Functionings can be univocally good (e.g., being in good health) or univocally bad (e.g., being raped). But the goodness or badness of various other functionings may not be so straightforward, but rather depend on the context and/or the normative theory we endorse.

In other words, the capability approach does not from the outset dictate which capabilities and functionings are morally relevant, whether for human development, justice, or any other domain. This underspecification and open-endedness has led capability theorists to argue that we need a selection of relevant capabilities and functionings when applying the concepts in practice (e.g., Fukuda-Parr 2003, 121; Sen 1989, 46). Selecting which capabilities and functionings are included on a list of development goals, meanwhile, raises two further questions, namely who should make the selection and how should they go about doing so?

Accordingly, the second question that I shall investigate in this book concerns *who* should select the relevant development goals for a development agenda. Since the largely donor- and expert-driven formulation of the MDGs in 2000, which set out the global development agenda for the following fifteen years, the fact that many developing countries have in the meantime shed their aid-dependency has ushered in a claim to grant local stakeholders greater authority in the process of setting a development agenda. In the third chapter of the book I shall investigate what I call *the claim to local authority*. As a working definition, I define the claim to local authority in the following way, which I will specify further in Chapters 3 and 4:

> *Local stakeholders should be granted greater authority in deciding on matters of development in general and especially in relation to development initiatives, such as a development agenda that they are affected by.*

In Chapter 3, I first argue that the claim to local authority underlies at least three prominent development concepts, namely empowerment, local development ownership, and indigenous knowledge, either implicitly or explicitly. For empowerment, local development ownership, and indigenous knowledge to make any sense as normative claims—that is, that local stakeholders *should* be empowered to take control of their own lives, that local stakeholders *should* be granted some degree of ownership of the development process, and that indigenous knowledge *should* play a bigger part in development debates—they need to include a claim to local authority.

Note that I am not advocating a full transfer of authority to local stakeholders. I am merely arguing that local stakeholders should be granted more authority in two ways. First, local stakeholders should be granted more authority, relatively speaking, as compared to their historical levels of authority—or lack thereof—in development matters, and this is therefore connected to the process of making local stakeholders agents of change rather than merely passive recipients of aid (Goulet 1971, 148; Sen 1999b, 11). Second, local stakeholders should be granted authority in an absolute sense to the extent that it satisfies certain criteria for democratic legitimacy as specified by the claim to local authority.

In the context of setting a development agenda, I argue that the claim to local authority should be interpreted as a claim to two kinds of authority, namely political authority and expert authority. On the one hand, the process of setting a development agenda is in many ways a political process in which different stakeholders come to a satisfactory consensus about what goals should be achieved by development efforts. As such, the claim to local authority is a claim for local stakeholders to have the political freedom to influence this process. I label this the claim to local political authority.

In Chapter 3, I further argue that the general idea of local political authority can be specified in four ways through republican theory. First, the claim to local political authority should be understood as the claim that local stakeholders should not be subject to domination, understood as the arbitrary exercise of power, in the political process of setting a development agenda from national policy-makers, external stakeholders, or fellow citizens. Second, the claim to local political authority holds that the political process of setting a development agenda should respect certain procedural constraints that restrict the extent to which power can be exercised, *not* that the development agenda must substantively represent the preferences and values of the local stakeholders. Third, I argue that local political authority is threatened by both public and private exercises of power, the regulation of which requires different strategies, such as a rule of law and socioeconomic policies and laws.

However, before a development agenda becomes a political question, it is processed within another domain, namely the domain of expertise, where different development experts provide input to the political process. As such, development experts have the authority to influence the development agenda. In this regard, the claim to local authority becomes a claim for local stakeholders to be granted such expert authority. In Chapter 4, I argue that local stakeholders can legitimately claim expert authority in matters concerning their own development insofar as they possess tacit or embodied knowledge that can meaningfully contribute to a development agenda. I label this view *third wave development expertise* to mark the difference between a first wave, positivist account of development expertise and a second wave, social constructivist approach.

One obstacle to local stakeholders' exercise of their expert authority lies in the fact that they often lack the ability to interact with established experts. (Similarly, established experts may also lack the ability to interact meaningfully with local stakeholders.) I argue that employing five types of experts who can mediate between local stakeholders, established experts, and political decision-makers can ameliorate this obstacle.

With the defense of local political authority and the introduction of third wave development expertise, the second question that I have set out to answer in this book will be answered. We still need to address the third fundamental question related to the establishment of a development agenda, namely *how* this process can play out: by which method(s) should we select capabilities and functionings for a development agenda? The claim to local authority—understood in terms of both republicanism and third wave development expertise—is compatible with a variety of approaches to the selection of capabilities and functionings. For example, quantitative and qualitative surveys of various kinds, public deliberations, and referenda, which involve politicians, development experts, and citizens, may all be ways of selecting and adopting a set of development goals.

As there are so many alternative methods, the third question I ask in this book is by which method we should select relevant capabilities and functionings for a development agenda. Several methods for the selection of capabilities and functionings have been proposed within the capability literature. In Chapter 6, I identify, analyze, and discuss fifteen such methods, which can be categorized into ad hoc, foundational, procedural, and mixed (or multi-stage) methods. Ad hoc methods base their selection of capabilities on ad hoc considerations, foundational methods on normative values and principles, and procedural methods on more open-ended, democratic information, while mixed (or multi-stage) methods employ foundational and procedural methods in conjunction.

Before I engage in an evaluation of these methods, I first identify, in Chapter 5, a set of criteria that a method used for the selection of capabilities and functionings should satisfy. On the basis of these criteria, I dismiss outright those methods that rely on ad hoc, purely foundational, or purely procedural methods for the selection of capabilities and functionings. Ad hoc methods are dismissed because of their lack of theoretical methodological and normative justification, and foundational methods due to a lack of democratic legitimacy and contextual sensitivity, while procedural methods are found to be vulnerable to implicit biases and adaptive preferences.

Rather, in Chapter 6, I argue that we should adopt a multi-stage method, which I label *synthesizing methods*. Synthesizing methods aim to engage critically with local stakeholders in a three-stage procedure. While the purpose of the first stage is to enrich the normative and descriptive theory through empirical and deliberative exercises, the second stage offers this refined theory as an input to a democratic procedure with the aim of enhancing the informational bases of the participants. Lastly, in the third stage, local stakeholders engage in a critical deliberation with an informed and widely endorsed list of capabilities and functionings as an ideal outcome.

Finally, I argue that for a synthesizing method to be successful in setting a development agenda, it should be supplemented by the five types of mediating experts that I identify in Chapter 4. The general role of the mediating experts is to mediate between local stakeholders, established experts, and political decision-makers in order to facilitate a deliberation on a development agenda, which brings together normative principles, empirical insights, and democratic concerns.

In sum, I argue for an inclusive framework for the setting of a development agenda, which includes the following three aspects.

- First, the goals of a development agenda are best conceptualized in terms of capabilities and functionings. Capabilities are the real freedom that people have to do or be certain things; functionings are capabilities that have been realized.
- Second, local stakeholders should be granted both political and expert authority in the setting of a development agenda. Politically, the claim to local authority is best accounted for with reference to republican theory, which safeguards local stakeholders against arbitrary domination, while expert authority is best granted to local stakeholders on the basis of their tacit or embodied knowledge about local socioeconomic and environmental conditions.
- Third, the best method for setting a development agenda is to follow a multi-stage process, which aims to foster critical engagement between different stakeholders, such as local agents, government policymakers, and external development experts. In order to facilitate this critical engagement, the process should be guided by a variety of mediating experts.

To anticipate, I acknowledge that there may be tensions between these three aspects that need to be addressed. The tensions are, in particular, (1) between the commitment to the capability framework and the commitment to grant local stakeholders authority in deciding on matters concerning their own development, (2) between the commitment to third wave development expertise and the commitment to republican political freedom, and (3) between the commitment to local political and expert authority and the commitment to a mixed method for the selection of capabilities. Where appropriate, I address these tensions in detail.

The tensions, as we shall see, cannot be completely avoided, but I take that to be an inherent part of embracing an integrated and inclusive approach to development, which takes different sources of input—that is, philosophical, anthropological, democratic—into account. This presents a number of challenges, such as differences between stakeholders in terms of power, influence, education, and status, as well as in terms of the normative status of substantive philosophical approaches vis-à-vis procedural approaches. Although these challenges cannot be completely avoided or addressed, I hope to show that they are, in fact, a vital part of development, understood as an ongoing dynamic process that must take into account and accommodate nonideal socioeconomic circumstances and different social and professional norms and viewpoints, in addition to principles of social justice. It is highly likely that all of these aspects will always be in some sort of tension with each other.

In sum, this book offers novel answers to three fundamental questions related to the task of setting a development agenda. What kinds of goals should the agenda include? Who should set the agenda? And how should they do so? Taken together, the answers I provide to these questions lead to the construction of an innovative framework, which integrates stakeholders at all levels as well as distinct methods for the selection of goals for a development agenda.

1.3 Concluding Remarks

The framework that I develop in this book addresses three fundamental questions that we need to ask before we can set a development agenda. The three fundamental questions ask what kinds of goals a development agenda should include, who should be involved in the setting of a development agenda, and by which method they should select relevant development goals. Because our answers to these three fundamental questions have the potential to influence the particular goals of our agenda, it becomes imperative that we can provide good reasons and arguments for them. This is the challenge that this book must meet. Throughout, I not only draw on well-established theories—such as the capability approach and republicanism—to support my framework, but also look to address the questions through approaches that can provide novel solutions to long-standing issues within the development literature.

Who is this book for? What is its intended readership? The subject and style of the book mean that it is primarily of interest for mainstream academics working on development and issues of development. In particular, the book is directed to scholars of development studies and development ethics, but also touches upon themes relevant for applied ethicists and empirical scientists working within the capability approach and/or human development as well as scholars of indigenous studies, philosophy of expertise, and social scientists working on political representation and deliberative democracy.

While a full overview of the framework for setting development agendas that I present in this book requires that one reads all of the seven chapters, some readers with more specific interests might find value in only reading some of the chapters. For example, readers primarily interested in the capability approach will do well to read Chapter 2 for a brief introduction to the capability framework and how it can be applied to the context of development. Readers familiar with the capability approach and interested in the issue of how to select capabilities (for development purposes or otherwise) can skip ahead to Chapters 5 and 6. Readers interested in the democratic rights of local stakeholders within development should focus on Chapter 3, while readers interested in how to integrate local and indigenous knowledge within development should focus on Chapter 4, for a discussion of how to conceptualize development expertise, and Chapter 6, for a discussion of what methodology best integrates the perspectives of local stakeholders.

The book might also be of interest—although to a more limited extent—to readers outside of academia, such as development practitioners and policy-makers who are interested in the more theoretical aspects of development. (Disclaimer: although parts of this book talk of indigenous knowledge and would be of interest to practitioners working with indigenous people, it is important to note that it is not written specifically for indigenous scholars and activists and does not directly engage with indigenous scholarship.) The introduction to the capability approach in Chapter 1 would be of interest to readers looking for a multidimensional approach to development. Policy-makers and practitioners working on local and indigenous rights would do well to read Chapters 2 and 3, which grant local stakeholders more authority in matters of development. Nonacademic readers who are interested in the methodological aspects of development would also find Chapter 6 of interest, which discusses the different methods for selecting development goals.

Should one wish to read an 'executive summary' of the book, a brief overview of the arguments presented in the five main chapters can be found in Chapter 7. That said, I hope that this introductory chapter has whetted the appetite of the reader and that he or she will read the every chapter. In the end, I hope to be able to award the reader's patience by providing a compelling framework for identifying development goals for future development agendas or at the very least to encourage development stakeholders—donors, experts, practitioners, and policy-makers—to carefully consider what they mean when they talk about development.

Note

1 The strategy used by the Gates foundation has also been labeled 'philanthrocapitalism' or 'venture philanthropy': the idea that the performance of development projects and actors (such as development organizations and NGOs) should be evaluated based on business metrics, such as efficiency, pay-off, and cost-benefit. For a critique of the Gates Foundation's aid strategy, see Bowman (2012) and Birn (2014). For a more extensive discussion of the virtues and disadvantages of this strategy in development aid, see Letts, Ryan, and Grossman (1997), Kramer (2002), Katz (2005), and McGoey (2012).

2 A Capability Framework for Development Goals

The world has seen unprecedented advances in the past one and a half centuries. Never has the amount of wealth in the world been greater (Credit Suisse 2013), and the average GDP per capita has been on the rise since the 1820s (van Zanden et al. 2014, chap. 3). Medical advances, such as better hygiene and the discoveries of penicillin, antibiotics, and vaccines, have had a profound effect on human health and longevity as well as significantly lowering the global infant mortality rates (Centers for Disease Control and Prevention 1999; van Zanden et al. 2014, chap. 6). We are now able to communicate effectively in a matter of seconds across the globe thanks to the surge in ICTs, something that previously would have taken days, weeks, or even months. The inventions of first steam power and later fossil fuels have facilitated transportation (Rodrigue and Comtois 2013), making it possible to circumnavigate the earth in a couple of days or to travel to Paris for business in the morning and return for dinner in your London suburb in the afternoon.

Despite all of these advances, there are still persistent inequalities in people's health, educational achievements, and social security. What is more, these inequalities have a tendency to further disadvantage the already disadvantaged—mainly children, females, and inhabitants of developing countries—who bear little responsibility for their situation. Child mortality, although halved since 1990, is still staggering, with the deaths of 6.3 million children under the age of five in 2013 (averaging 17,000 children *per day*) according to a recent report by the UN Inter-agency Group for Child Mortality Estimation (2014, 1). The International Programme on the Elimination of Child Labour (IPEC) (2013, vii) estimates that "168 million children worldwide are in child labour, accounting for almost 11 per cent of the child population as a whole," half of which (85 million) are working under hazardous conditions directly endangering their health and safety. Women's education is still not a priority in many societies (although it has been moved to the center of much development thinking) and, according to UNESCO, two-thirds of all illiterate adults are women (UNESCO Institute for Statistics 2014). And the Intergovernmental Panel on Climate Change reports that the inhabitants of least-developed countries are especially vulnerable to climate changes due to the lack of socioeconomic security (IPCC 2014; see also Warner et al. 2013).[1]

These inequalities raise the first fundamental question that I shall answer in this book: what kind of development discourse should guide our efforts to set a development agenda? What kind of discourse best captures the challenges that development faces, and what kinds of goals does it entail? In this chapter, I argue that a development agenda is best conceptualized in terms of the concept of *human development*. Human development holds that the kinds of goals that a development agenda should include are best conceptualized in terms of capabilities and functionings. Capabilities are the real freedom that people have to do or be certain things; functionings are capabilities that have been realized. I further argue that adopting the human development and capability framework has, on the one hand, significant benefits over any of its alternative discourses. On the other hand, the chapter explicates the unique challenges that need to be addressed and accommodated when setting a development agenda based on a commitment to the human development and capability framework.

The chapter is structured as follows. In the first section (2.1), I argue that we should conceptualize development goals in terms of capabilities and functionings and proceed to introduce the capability approach, its terms, concepts, and normative commitments. In section 2.2, I show how the capability framework provides a basis for conceptualizing development goals in terms of human development. In section 2.3, I specify my account of human development and argue that we should prefer a hybrid approach, which holds that a development agenda should focus on both basic and advanced capabilities or functionings. Section 2.4 considers what issues we need to be aware of when setting a development agenda based on the human development and capability framework while the final section (2.5) dispels the objection that the commitment to the capability approach is in tension with the commitment to local authority that will be defended in the subsequent chapters.

2.1 A Short Introduction to the Capability Approach

How we shape our development agenda often depends on the kind of development ethics that we subscribe to. Development ethics is the interdisciplinary field of studies concerning the ends and means of local, national, and international development (Astroulakis 2011, 100; Crocker 1991, 457). What, development ethicists ask, is normatively important in development? What should development achieve and how should it go about doing so? In other words, development ethics brings normative values to the discipline of development economics. It concerns the *oughts* and *shoulds* of the theory and practice of development. How should we conceptualize development? What ought we do to realize development? Who should benefit from and who should be responsible for development?

A major question within development ethics concerns what kinds of goals we should pursue as a matter of development. In this section, I argue that we should adopt the concept of human development when setting a development agenda. According to human development, development goals should be conceptualized in terms of capabilities and functionings. I provide an introduction to the capability framework, including its core concepts—such as capabilities and functionings—and its normative commitments before I show how it provides basis for human development.

In recent years, the capability approach has not only become increasingly influential in academia but also within debates on global, national, and local socioeconomic policy (Robeyns 2006, 351–2; Pressman and Summerfield 2002). In addition to providing the conceptual foundations for the UNDP's Human Development Index in the early 1990s, capability scholars have in the last decade been involved in commissions offering policy advice to the governments of both France and Germany (Stiglitz et al. 2010; Volkert 2005).

The idea of human development has been largely influenced by the capability approach, which has been advanced by a large number of scholars, most prominently Amartya Sen and Martha Nussbaum.[2] The capability approach has its origins in a number of articles in which Sen criticizes the limited informational bases of the traditional economic models and evaluative accounts (i.e., utilitarianism and resourcism).[3] What is missing from these traditional models, Sen argues, is a notion of what activities we are able to undertake ('doings') and the kinds of persons we are able to be ('beings'). Sen calls this notion *capabilities*.[4] Capabilities are the *real freedoms* that people have to achieve their potential doings and beings. Real freedom in this sense means that one has all the required means necessary to achieve that doing and being if one wishes to. That is, it is not merely the formal freedom to do or be something, but the substantial opportunity to achieve it.

Someone might, for example, have the formal freedom to vote in elections in the sense that she has a right to do so and that no one will stop her from doing so, but she might lack the substantial possibility to vote because the closest voting station is 200 kilometers away and she does not own a car and does not have access to other means of transportation. Conversely, someone may be living close to the voting station but still may not have the real freedom to vote because females are not permitted to vote in that particular society. Capabilities are thus real freedoms in the sense that they are corrected for any potential impediments. *Functionings* simply denotes those capabilities that have been achieved whether voluntarily or by chance. For example, someone might have the real freedom to vote but chooses not to do so and thus does not have the functioning of voting.

It is important to notice that capabilities and functionings can be both positive and negative, as well as neutral (Robeyns 2016). Thus, examples of 'doings' are to eat, travel, fall in love, read the phone book, pollute, and rape. Example of 'beings' are being altruistic, being in good health, being educated, being criminal, and being raped. All capabilities of one person taken together are referred to as her *capability set*. Although most applications of the capability approach focus on people's positive capabilities—what we consider *valuable* for them to do or be—we may also sometimes want to consider their negative capabilities. For example, it matters to the evaluation of a person's well-being or standard of living whether she is at risk of being murdered or being raped, which are both what we would call negative capabilities insofar as we consider them *not* to be valuable. Hence, in order to capture the variety of applications of the capability framework, it is important that the concepts of capabilities and functionings are kept value-neutral. If capabilities and functionings only encompassed positively valued doings and beings, we would not be able to capture the relevance of negative doings and beings (such as being murdered or being raped) for a person's well-being.

The capability approach changes the focus from means (the resources[5] people have) to ends (what they are able to do and be with those resources and goods). This shift in focus is justified because resources and goods alone do not ensure that people are able to convert them into actual doings and beings. Two persons with similar sets of goods and resources may be able to achieve very different ends depending on their circumstances. One of the most prominent illustrations within the capability literature of the need to move beyond a focus on goods and resources is found in Sen's (1979a) *Equality of What?* Here, Sen asks us to consider two persons with the same amount of resources. One, however, suffers from a disability. This disability makes her unequal to the able-bodied person in two regards, which cannot be captured by a sole focus on resources. First of all, the disabled person is unequal in terms of what she can do with her resources compared with the physically able person. She may, for example, be confined to a wheelchair and thus restricted to places with wheelchair access. Second, the disabled person may even be doubly worse off because she only gets the same amount of resources even though she has more expenses in order to correct for her disability. That is, because the disabled person needs to spend a considerable amount of her resources on a wheelchair merely to move around, she actually has fewer resources available to pursue other goals than the able-bodied person who, *ex hypothesi*, can spend all her resources toward pursuing her valued ends. Thus, in order to evaluate people's well-being, we need to not only consider the amount of resources they have but also what they are able to do and be with those resources.

Moreover, what Sen's example shows is that the conversion of resources and goods into capabilities and/or functionings crucially relies on various *conversion factors*. Conversion factors are the conditions that influence a person's ability to exploit the value of some resource, good, or formal freedom that one has. The *real* value of a bicycle, for example, depends on whether the person in question has the mental and physical skills to ride the bicycle (personal conversion factors), whether the relevant laws and social norms allow her to ride the bicycle (social conversion factors), and whether there are decent roads and an adequate infrastructure (environmental conversion factors). The *real freedom* someone has to ride a bicycle is thus dependent on whether these conditions are fulfilled. In this sense, conversion factors also shape the *needs* of the individuals in question: in a society in which the capability of riding a bicycle is important (e.g., in order to get to work), it becomes crucial to provide decent roads and an adequate infrastructure (Crocker and Robeyns 2010, 68).

Human beings are diverse. Our well-being depends on our ability to fulfill our needs, yet both our needs and our ability to fulfill them differ depending on our personal and contextual circumstances. That is, people get different amounts of well-being from the same set of resources depending on the conversion factors they are subject to. To illustrate, recall the example of the disabled individual mentioned earlier. Arguably, the disabled individual requires more resources—qua being disabled—in order to experience the same increase in well-being as her able-bodied peers.

A utilitarian may argue, however, that this only shows that we ought to distribute *more* resources, goods, and freedoms to the disabled person to the extent that she experiences the same amount of well-being as the able-bodied person. As Sen (1979a) has shown, however, this response is inadequate. The disabled person may be a pleasure wizard who gains a lot of utility from very little input. Conversely, the able-bodied person may be very hard to please and thus requires a large input of resources and freedoms in order to detect an increase in well-being. In this case, Sen notes, the amended utilitarian position would actually direct more resources and freedoms to the able-bodied person and less to the disabled one. But surely it cannot be right to provide less help to those with greater needs, merely because they are easier to satisfy. As Sen himself has documented, people in poor conditions may actually tend to lower their expectations and settle into their poverty (e.g., Kynch and Sen 1983). But just because they experience a bigger increase in well-being from fewer resources does not mean that the situation is justified or justifiable in the first place.

A concept of well-being should thus recognize the diversity of human needs and personal and contextual circumstances. This is exactly what the notions of capabilities and functionings do. First, by focusing on what people are able to do and be (rather than on an equal distribution of goods and resources), the capability approach recognizes the diversity of people's ability to convert those resources and goods into real opportunities and achievements. Second, Sen distinguishes between two kinds of freedom, namely what he calls *well-being freedom* and *agency freedom* (Sen 1985). Both of these can also be analyzed in terms of whether they have been achieved. In this case they are called *well-being achievement* and *agency achievement*. Well-being freedoms are those freedoms that promote our well-being generally. Being well nourished, for example, is a part of our well-being. But we may also value freedoms that do not promote our well-being, such as giving up a promising career in order to fight for global justice. My fighting for global justice may not provide me with anything in terms of well-being, as it requires me to travel to some of the most insecure places on earth and does not provide a steady income. I am worse off in terms of well-being compared to the alternative of pursuing a promising career. Yet I value this freedom because it is an expression of my agency.[6] The recognition of agency freedom, in addition to well-being freedom, allows people to pursue a diversity of doings and beings.

What particular capabilities and functionings are normatively relevant? The first thing we should notice is that the commitment to consider the diversity of human needs and circumstances has often led capability scholars to argue that we need to make a selection of capabilities and functionings depending on the particular domain of application and/or the particular socioeconomic context. In the first case, as argued, the capability approach can be applied to many more specific domains, such as a capability theory of justice, empirical studies, the evaluation of social policies, the design of development initiatives, and so on. Each of these domains of application may require different lists of capabilities. In the second case, the commitment to human diversity should lead us to acknowledge that which capabilities are normatively relevant may differ both between individuals and between societies.

It should be noted that some scholars have argued that all capabilities are valuable and, hence, that there is no need to make a selection of normatively relevant capabilities. This view can especially be attributed to Carter (2014) and Vallentyne (2005). Carter's and Vallentyne's views are outliers, however, and almost all capability scholars agree that we need to make a selection of normatively relevant capabilities and functionings. In this book, I shall proceed on the assumption that we need to make a selection of capabilities and functionings when applying the capability approach in practice, for example in order to set a development agenda. In Chapters 5 and 6, I investigate the issue of selecting capabilities and functionings in more detail, including *why* we need to make a selection.

The proliferation of literature on the capability approach has engendered a discussion about how to exactly define it. While Nussbaum (2011b) seems to provide an elaborate account of the entire capability framework,

Robeyns (2016, 2017) has recently argued that this account cannot constitute the definitive version of the capability approach. Rather, Robeyns argues that we can define the capability approach more minimally than Nussbaum does. The capability approach, Robeyns argues, should be defined as a normative framework, which can host a wide variety of more specific theories and applications, such as, for example, Nussbaum's partial capability theory of justice, Crocker's capability theory of deliberative democracy, or Kuklys's capabilitarian econometrics (Robeyns 2016). Likewise, Qizilbash (2012) argues that the capability approach should be seen as a 'thin' framework, which can be filled in by 'thicker' theories and applications.

While all of these accounts may differ greatly in their specific structure, purpose, and normative commitments, they all adhere to the same normative core. Thus, at the center of the capability framework, Robeyns (2016, 2017) argues, is a normative commitment to conceptualize well-being in terms of capabilities and functionings—the real freedom that people have to do or be certain things. In this way, Robeyns provides an account of the capability approach that both pays due respect to the variety of work being done on or with the approach and manages to define its core in concise principles.

2.2 Development as the Expansion of Capabilities and Functionings

One of the domains that the capability framework can be applied to is development, where it has given birth to the development discourse known as *human development*.[7] Human development is the idea that processes of development should benefit the people whom they affect by expanding what they are able to do or be with their resources (Streeten 1994, 232; Qizilbash 1996, 144).[8] The ideal of human development arose out of a discontent with the fact that existing development paradigms, such as economic growth and human resource development, would often bring about social injustices or fail to enhance people's actual well-being (Qizilbash 1996, 143). Whereas both of these paradigms only consider human beings as the *means* to economic growth, the idea of human development holds that the primary *end* of development should be people (Haq 1996, 5).[9]

In other words, the focus should, according to human development, be on what people are able to do and be with their resources rather than with the resources themselves. Maximizing economic growth is thus, on this view, only a means to achieve development insofar as it enhances people's capabilities—their opportunity to do and be certain things. Consider, again, the value of a bicycle. From the perspective of an economic growth paradigm, the value of the bicycle is either intrinsic—insofar as it is a product of economic wealth—or instrumental as a means to create economic growth (e.g., by transporting laborers to and from work). From the perspective of a human resource development paradigm, the bicycle has instrumental value because it allows someone to get to work (and contribute to economic production). The idea of human development holds that the bicycle has instrumental value only insofar as it expands the owner's freedom to lead a flourishing life regardless of whether this leads to a rise in economic growth.

Several scholars have argued that human development is essentially a pluralistic concept (Alexander 2004; Drydyk 2011; Haq 1996, 14–16; Nussbaum 2003; Sen 2005). This is so in three ways. First, there are several capabilities that are important for human development. Education, health, nourishment, shelter, and security are only some of the most basic capabilities, but we may also value more 'advanced' capabilities such as traveling, reading a good book, being physically active, going to the movies, taking care of one's sick mother, fighting for global justice, voting in a democratic election, being a good parent, and participating in a community (Robeyns 2011). It is of course possible that the value of all of these capabilities may differ between two persons or from one society to another. Someone who leads an adventurous lifestyle, for example, may have less need for security than most people.

Second, we may need different means to achieve our capabilities. This is not only due to the fact that we may value different capabilities but also because the same capability may be realized through different means. Consider, for example, how the functioning of traveling may be achieved through different means of transportation, such as by car, train, plane, and bike, or on foot. The idea of human development thus holds that neither the ends nor the means of development can be reduced to a single dimension. Third, the obstacles we face in achieving human development are diverse, as exemplified by Sen's three conversion factors. These personal, social, and environmental factors are the conditions that enable or restrict someone's use of a tangible or intangible good. Someone may be unable to vote in the elections either because it is illegal for women to vote in her society (a social conversion factor) or because she is severely disabled (a personal conversion factor) and cannot get to the voting station.

Although human development and the notions of capabilities and functionings provide us with a *theoretically* stronger alternative to other development paradigms, as argued, we still need to ask to what extent does it correspond with what local stakeholders value or find important in development? This becomes especially important when we turn to answer the second question of this book in Chapters 3 and 4, namely the extent to which local stakeholders should be involved in the selection of development goals. What if, we need to ask, local stakeholders, when granted influence in this regard, prefer to conceptualize development in terms of some other concept of 'advantage' or well-being, such as economic growth, resources, or happiness? Is the capability framework compatible with letting people decide on matters concerning their own development, or do the commitments of the capability approach to a specific conceptualization of well-being silence local values, preferences, and knowledge?[10]

There is empirical evidence that local stakeholders do conceptualize their own ends in terms of capabilities and functionings. One of the most comprehensive surveys of people's values and ends are the three *Voices of the Poor* reports, published at the turn of the millennium (Narayan et al. 1999, 2000; Narayan and Petesch 2002). Featuring interviews with more than 60,000 poor individuals from around the world, what the reports reveal is that those interviewed often frame and describe their circumstances, goals, ambitions, and aspirations in terms of what they are (or would like to be) able to do or be; that is, in terms of capabilities and functionings. Even when asked about the value of material goods and resources, those interviewed expressed the view that "the material is only one dimension among others" and primarily as a means to other ends (Narayan et al. 2000, 24). As noted earlier, Alkire (2002) reaches the same conclusion after asking the participants in three development projects to evaluate the outcomes of the projects. What they valued was not so much the economic outcome (that was often marginal or non-existent) as much as what the projects enabled them to do or be, such as being literate, forming social relationships, or influencing household decisions.

However, based on his fieldwork in a South African context, Clark (2005) found that while locals did indeed value 'traditional' sources of well-being, such as being clothed, having good housing, and being able to engage in physical activity, respondents also contradicted the capability framework in two ways. In the first case, Clark's respondents, when asked what they valued, also included both material goods (clothing, television) and mental pleasures (the joy of watching sports) on their lists. In the second case, the respondents valued having capabilities, which we would traditionally consider negative or at least nonpositive, such as smoking tobacco or drinking Coca-Cola and alcohol.

What are we to make of Clark's findings vis-à-vis the capability framework? The first thing we should notice is that in both cases what the respondents value can be interpreted as proxies for other (positive) capabilities or functionings. For example, in relation to the first case, when asked *why* they valued having the material good of a television, the respondents highlighted its value as a means to other capabilities, such as learning new things and facilitating social life (Clark 2005, 1356). In relation to the second case, the seemingly nonvaluable capability of drinking Coca-Cola[11] was described as a proxy for access to clean drinking water and medical remedies to relieve stomachache, flatulence, and diarrhea (Clark 2005, 1352). These findings point to the idea that if we inquire enough into the reasons why people value something, we may be able to describe it in terms of some positive capability.

That said, according to Clark, even at this level of inquiry many respondents still expressed the value of certain items on the list in terms of their mental pleasure. For example, in addition to being seen as a means to status, prestige, and physical fitness, the capability of playing sports was also valued because of the pleasure that the respondents got from its exercise. While the focus on mental states, pleasure, and happiness is not incompatible with the capability approach—"[h]appiness may be a valuable part of well-being"—it "cannot serve as a surrogate" for well-being (Sen 1985a, 200). Clark's findings, however, show that we need to consider the mental pleasure that people derive from a certain functioning as an intrinsic part of why people value that functioning. Moreover, Clark (2005, 1360–61; italics in original) argues that his findings show that the capability framework must also focus on resources and commodities because "a person needs a *combination* of commodities before s/he can achieve specific functionings satisfactorily" and "[i]t is unlikely that any combination of relevant inputs will do." To wit, even if we focus on people's capabilities and functionings, we need to also focus at least partly on securing the *right* commodities and resources that are necessary for people to have these capabilities and functionings.

In sum, I have in this section given an introduction to the human development and capability approach. The human development and capability approach is normatively committed to the idea that development goals should be relative to individual, socioeconomic, and environmental circumstances and introduces several concepts—capabilities and functionings, conversion factors, well-being, and agency freedom—that can help capture and conceptualize development as basic requirements for human life but also as the freedom to pursue personal aspirations and ends above the basic threshold. The framework provided by the human development and capability approach, as I have presented it here, gives us an answer to the first question I set out in the introduction to this book, namely what *kinds* of goals should we include on a development agenda? The answer provided makes it clear that we would do well to conceptualize the goals of a development agenda in terms of capabilities and functionings—what people are able to do and be.

One issue remains to be investigated. Should a development agenda include basic capabilities, basic functionings, advanced capabilities, and advanced functionings, or a combination of two or more of these, or all of them? In the following section, I argue for the last option, namely that a development agenda should consist of basic and advanced capabilities and functionings.

2.3 Specifying Human Development as a Hybrid Position

A human development discourse holds that development should promote the doings and beings that people have reason to value, lead to a flourishing life, or that are somehow just or virtuous. Two questions remain unanswered, however. First, should the goals focus on basic capabilities and/or functionings or advanced capabilities and/or functionings?[12] Second, should the goals of a development agenda focus on achieved doings and being (i.e., functionings) or rather the real freedom to pursue these doings and beings (i.e., capabilities)? In this section, I argue that a development agenda needs to include goals that represent a combination of basic and advanced capabilities and functionings. I first deal with the first question and argue that while development cannot be reduced to a concern with basic capabilities and functionings, we do need to include certain basic capabilities and functionings as preconditions for more advanced capabilities and functionings. I then turn to the second question and argue that although a pure functionings approach is problematic because it ignores human agency, we nevertheless need to include certain achieved functionings. This is so for two reasons: first, because some basic achievements are necessary in order to pursue capabilities in the first place and, second, because we may need some individuals to fulfill certain functionings (e.g., paying their taxes) in order to ensure the capabilities of other individuals.

2.3.1 Basic or Advanced Doings and Beings?

An important distinction made within the capability literature is between basic capabilities (and functionings) and advanced capabilities (and functionings). The term *basic capabilities*, as I shall use it, refers to the idea that we need to ensure a minimum threshold of capabilities and functionings, for example, in order for people to survive, flourish properly, or have sufficient agential capacity.

While some doings and beings are widely recognized as necessary for human survival—for example, access to food and adequate health care—a list of basic capabilities and functionings can also include other doings and beings that are central to human life although not to survival. Nussbaum (2011a, 33–4), for example, includes on her list of central capabilities and functionings not only life and bodily health but also mental capabilities, such as having emotions and an imagination, as well as social capabilities, such as being able to engage in social relations with fellow humans and other species. Such doings and beings, Nussbaum (1992) argues, are essential to humans. That is, without them, we would hesitate to call it a *human* life. Because basic capabilities and functionings (however specified) are so central to human life, some scholars have argued that we have a duty to provide them to everyone as a matter of justice or human rights (Nussbaum 2011b; Vizard 2007; Arneson 2005).

In my criticism of the basic needs development discourse, I argued that a focus on basic needs ignores the fact that human beings have aspirations that go beyond the satisfaction of their basic requirements. The main problem with a sole focus on basic capabilities and functionings is that it does not consider doings and beings that are not essential for human life yet may be valuable or relevant in a human development perspective. I refer to such nonessential capabilities (and functionings) as *advanced capabilities*. For example, having the opportunity to become a graduate student would not be considered essential or a threshold requirement to human life (whether it is defined in terms of survival, flourishing, or agential capacity) in most parts of the world. We would still be able to survive and function properly in most aspects of life with a lower degree of education. Yet we might still consider it to be normatively relevant for human development because someone who has access to graduate school is arguably better off than someone who does not.

Scholars who stress the need to go beyond basic doings and beings and include more advanced capabilities and functionings often stress the value of freedom of choice and agency within the capability approach (Crocker and Robeyns 2010). That is, as argued, people have a variety of agential aspirations and life goals that cannot necessarily be reduced to a set of basic capabilities. Following Sen (1985), we can refer to this as the *agency aspect* of development. In order to capture the agency aspect of development we may need to ensure that people have access to a wider range of advanced doings and beings that present them with choices between different lifestyles, such as whether or not to attend graduate school. Again, which doings and beings are relevant in this sense may differ between both individuals and societies and is thus a question that must be addressed in consultation with the local stakeholders, as I shall argue in the subsequent chapters.

In sum, both basic and advanced doings and beings can have normative relevance for development. On the one hand, as Nussbaum (2000, 84) points out, the pursuit of more advanced capabilities requires that certain basic doings and beings are available or achieved. Human development, however, does not only concern the threshold requirements of human life but also the range of opportunities that individual agents can choose from. Insofar as we need to capture this agency aspect of development and socioeconomic progress, we ought to include more advanced doings and beings on our development agenda. Consequently, a development agenda needs to incorporate both basic and advanced doings and beings that are (normatively) relevant.

2.3.2 *Capabilities or Functionings?*

The second specification we need to make concerns whether a development agenda should focus on achievement (i.e., functionings) or rather on real opportunities (i.e., capabilities). I argue first that the agency aspect of development requires us to at least include certain capabilities on a development agenda. However, I also argue that there are two reasons why we need to include a focus on certain functionings: first, because some basic achievements are necessary in order to pursue capabilities in the first place and, second, because we may need to restrict the freedom of some people in order to ensure the freedom of other individuals.

Why ought we to focus a development agenda on capabilities rather than functionings? The primary reason for a focus on capabilities is the concern with agency and people's freedom to pursue their own valued lifestyles. Capabilities present people with certain real opportunities, which they can choose to realize or not. A focus on functionings, on the contrary, is engaged in developing certain lifestyles rather than promoting people's freedom to pursue their own valued lifestyles. Obviously, such achievements could be in securing that people have basic functionings such as being healthy, nourished, and secure. In that case, a functionings approach is similar to the basic needs approach to development. But a functionings approach can also focus on achieving more advanced functionings, such as a higher level of democratic or community participation or greener and more sustainable lifestyles.

The worry here is that a focus on functionings entails a particular view of the good life (Claassen 2014, 60–1; Robeyns 2011). Not only is any account of the good life likely to be controversial given the diversity of human aspirations, but basing development on such an account also justifies widespread paternalistic interventions with people's choices, which is likely to violate the commitment to agency freedom (Carter 2014; Claassen 2014).[13] Consider, for example, how a particularly Western ideal has guided much development practice and the extent to which these practices have sought to 'civilize' the 'savage' peoples of the non-Western world.[14] Of course, a view of the good life does not necessarily need to have such colonial overtones, but we need to focus, at least partially, on people's opportunities—rather than achievements—because of the intrinsic value that we may put on the freedom to choose between alternative paths in life.

There are good reasons why we should also focus our development agenda on achieved functionings, however. Of course, there are special cases where we need to promote certain functionings because the individuals concerned are not able to choose, such as infants and children, the severely mentally disabled, and individuals suffering from dementia and brain damage. As Robeyns (2011) argues, "it is generally held that we (through families, governments, or other institutions) have the moral obligation to promote or protect their nutritional and healthy functioning." Beyond such special cases, meanwhile, we can identify two instances where we need to focus on functionings. Let me consider each in turn.

First, we may need to secure a certain threshold of functioning in order to be able to pursue capabilities in the first place (Claassen 2014, 63–8; Nussbaum 2000, 89–93).[15] The promotion of (some) functionings may therefore be an unavoidable instrumental step in the promotion of capabilities (Claassen 2014, 63). As Nussbaum (2000, 89–90;

see also Nussbaum 2006, 171–3 and Claassen 2014, 63–4) argues, "[i]f we aim to produce adults who have all the capabilities on the list, this will frequently mean requiring certain types of functioning in children." Nussbaum (2000, 92) puts special emphasis on two functionings that are instrumentally central to people's ability to act agentially, namely affiliation and practical reason, which "suffuse all other the capabilities, making them fully human." That is, affiliation and practical reason are supportive of our ability to exercise other capabilities. For example, we exercise the functioning of practical reason when choosing which capabilities to pursue. Claassen (2014, 66), meanwhile, argues "that, to a certain extent, cross-linkages can be identified between almost all of the capabilities on Nussbaum's list," not only between practical reason and affiliation. For example, the functioning to move around freely seems to be a precondition for participating in political decision-making, which is an instance of the capability to control one's environment.[16] If this is true, we need to include at least some threshold for such supportive functionings.

The second reason why a partial focus on functionings is necessary derives from the observation that we may need to limit which capabilities and functionings some individuals are able to pursue in order to ensure the freedom of other individuals, either at present or for future generations (Basu 1987, 74; Holland 2008; Watene 2013). Consider, for example, how everyone in a society may have the capability of accessing a social security system with free (or subsidized) health care and unemployment benefits but only insofar as everyone (or the majority) in that society realize the functioning of paying their share of the taxes. We may not want to include the individual functioning of paying taxes on a development agenda, but insofar as we find it normatively important that people have access to an effective social security system, we may want to include the functioning that people have such access, whether it is in the form of public or private services (only the former may require that taxes are paid).

In the second case, we may want to limit which capabilities people living at present have or can pursue in order to ensure that future generations have the same level or a minimal threshold of capabilities. Proponents of sustainable development in particular can argue that this requires present generations to achieve the functioning of living in a manner that is environmentally sustainable[17] because future generations also need natural resources to sustain a decent standard of living. However, we are currently depleting the earth's resources at an unsustainable rate. Furthermore, our current consumption of certain resources—most notably fossil fuels, such as coal, oil, and natural gas—threatens to change the earth's atmosphere to the extent that it will have an impact on the lives of future generation. For example, the release of CO_2 into the atmosphere, which occurs through the burning of coal, oil, and natural gas, has been shown to lead to global warming, indirectly causing desertification (and a lack of land suitable for agriculture), rising sea levels (and the threat of flooding and, especially in the case of small island development states, the loss of homes), volatile weather conditions, and the loss of rainforests. If we hold that development ought to be normatively concerned with future generations, we would do well to include such sustainability functionings—the functioning of living a green lifestyle—on our development agenda.[18]

In sum, in this section I have argued that our development agenda cannot be reduced to a singular concern with, on the one hand, either merely basic or advanced doings and beings and, on the other hand, only capabilities or only functionings. To the contrary, there are good reasons why a development agenda should be normatively concerned with both basic and advanced doings and beings as well as certain capabilities and functionings. I have called this a hybrid position on human development. A hybrid position on human development requires a selection of capabilities and functionings to consider the interplay between basic and advanced capabilities and functionings. In the final section of this chapter, I consider what particular characteristics of human development, as I have presented it in the previous sections, we need to be especially aware of when setting our development agenda.

2.4 Four Characteristics of Human Development Goals

In the previous sections, I have argued that we should conceptualize a development agenda in terms of human development and capabilities. I am now able to offer an account of human development goals that will be used throughout this book. In the following subsection, I ask: What does this commitment to human development and capabilities entail for the way in which we construct our development agenda? What should we be aware of when selecting goals for a development agenda? In other words, what characteristics do we ascribe to *human development goals*?

In this section, I finally summarize four characteristics that our development goals ought to embody.[19] First, human development is the idea that development issues arise because people are deprived of the opportunity to do or be certain valuable things and thus our development goals should involve a concern for people's agency. Second, human development goals should involve multiple stakeholders at multiple levels. Human development can be addressed as part of global development policy, as well as in a local context; human development deprivations not only occur in poor countries but also affect people in more affluent societies. Third, human development goals should be multidimensional in that they cannot be reduced to the improvement of one factor, such as economic growth or education, nor to the basic requirements of human life. Fourth, the circumstances surrounding human development issues are decidedly nonideal. Human development needs to be formulated against the background of a world where resources are limited, educational levels vary, economic inequalities are on the rise, and access to democratic institutions is restricted for a large part of its population, and a development agenda should reflect this.

2.4.1 A Concern with Human Agency

The first characteristic of human development goals is that they should be concerned with *human agency*.[20] Human development recognizes that development and well-being should be conceptualized in terms of the things people are able to do and be (i.e., their capabilities and functionings). In other words, it holds that development concerns the opportunities and freedom people have to exercise their agency. Setting a development agenda based on human development thus requires sensitivity to human agency. To illustrate, famines, as Sen (1980) has shown, constitute a human development issue because they are brought about as a consequence of a deprivation in people's capability to influence distributive policies or search out other sources of food. A famine, Sen argues, is a consequence of deprivations in human agency in areas other than a shortage of food. Human development thus relates to human agency in two ways. On the one hand, human development is about expanding the opportunities people have to exercise their agency. That is, human development policies and interventions should expand the capabilities people have to do and be certain things. In expanding people's capabilities, human agency is the primary end of development processes. On the other hand, human development interventions need to respect human beings as agents in the *process* of development. That is, human agents should not only be at the receiving end of development processes but should also be allowed to take part in them.

2.4.2 Multiple Stakeholders at Multiple Levels

The second characteristic we should ascribe to human development goals is that they involve *multiple stakeholders at multiple levels*. Someone's capability-deprivation is often brought about as a consequence of the actions of others, whether they are specific individuals, government policy-makers, or global institutions. Even if someone's capability set is restricted due to personal factors (e.g., poor health or mental capacities) what makes it a capability-deprivation is often a lack of accommodation by the surrounding society. A wheelchair only (or primarily) becomes a restriction for someone's free movement insofar as society fails to facilitate adequate wheelchair access. In turn, this failure may be a consequence of a lack of pressure on national policy-makers by international development institutions. Thus, human development issues can arise as a consequence of actions on multiple levels—personal, societal, national, and global—by a variety of different agents with different aims. Human development goals, as a consequence, must reflect this multitude of causes and stakeholders.

2.4.3 *Multidimensionality*

Likewise, third, human development goals should be *multidimensional*.[21] This is so in two ways. First, a human development issue can rarely be reduced to a deprivation of a single capability. As above, surrounding social and environmental factors most influence the gravity of someone's disability (a personal capability-deprivation). For example, a disability is worsened if the bearer at the same time lacks the capability to demand respect for her predicament, which could lead to the implementation of disability-friendly policies. Second, human development issues are multidimensional in the sense that they cannot be reduced to merely the basic requirements of human life, such as access to food, shelter, and security. Rather, human development is concerned with situations that are not only a matter of life and death. Consider, for example, the idea of human dignity, highlighted by Nussbaum (2000, chap. 4) as a core aim of capability development. Whether someone is able to live with dignity is hardly a matter of life and death. Yet we would not hesitate to say that dignity is crucial to living a flourishing (or even decent) life. Human development, unlike the basic needs approach, concerns more than the minimal and essential aspects of human life.

2.4.4 *Sensitivity to Nonideal Circumstances*

Human development issues arise as a consequence of *nonideal circumstances* and can only be solved with the help of nonideal measures. Accordingly, development goals should reflect this nonideal nature of development. We live in a world where resources are scarce, the global environment is changing, socioeconomic inequality is widespread, and democratic processes often prove inefficient, to mention just a few of the problems that humanity is facing. All of these factors are instrumental in creating human development deprivations, or are themselves deprivations. Being nonideal, these circumstances put pressure on us to intervene. New resources will not magically appear by themselves, global warming will not reverse unless interrupted, power relations will tend to reproduce socioeconomic inequalities, and democratic processes will continue to face issues of biases and affiliations. What is more, we cannot wait around for the perfect solution to address these issues. Just as Buridan's donkey starved to death trying to decide between two equally good haystacks, human development issues are too pressing to simply wait for ideal circumstances to arise. As Sen (2009) argues, in the face of the pressure human development deprivations puts on us to act, it is better to act using nonideal measures than to strive for that illusive ideal solution.

2.5 Concluding Remarks

In this chapter, I have answered the first question that I set out in the introduction to this book. I have argued that the goals of a development agenda are best conceptualized in terms of capabilities and functionings. Capabilities are the real freedom people have to do or be certain valuable things; functionings are capabilities that have been achieved. I have further argued that there are good reasons to include goals that are constitutive of the basic conditions of human life as well as goals that represent more advanced agential ends. A major consequence of this shift in focus is that we cannot immediately know which capabilities and functionings are normatively relevant for development. In setting a development agenda, then, we need to engage in a selection of relevant capabilities and functionings. In the following two chapters (3 and 4), I answer the second question that I raised for this book: Who should be involved in setting a development agenda? How and to what extent can we justify involving local stakeholders in the decision-making on their own development?

Notes

1 Conversely, the report by the IPCC (2014) also shows that more affluent countries are better able to adapt to the adverse effects of climate change.

2 Sen's particular capability theory has often been accused of being incomplete and underspecified. Gasper (2002), for example, correctly argues that the capability approach must be specified in a number of respects, such as the concepts of agency and need, in order to be able to address development issues. Because, in this book, I am merely interested in developing a framework that can be used to develop a particular human development agenda, I shall merely insist that making these specifications is a task for the particular human development theory.

3 For more on Sen's work on informational bases and his critiques of utilitarianism, resourcism, and welfarism, see, for example, Sen (1974, 1979a, 1979b, 1979c).

4 It should be noted that Sen in earlier texts used the term 'capabilities' to refer to a person's set of basic capabilities, rather than particular capabilities. Only later did he use the term in the broader sense of doings and beings. See also Robeyns (2011).

5 I shall use the term 'resources' here in its broader sense to denote material assets, as well as more intangible assets such as human capital, legal freedoms, and so on. Please note that on the most plausible reading of Sen (1985a), he is concerned with the conversion of more tangible resources. There is no reason, however, that we should not be equally concerned with the conversion of more intangible resources, such as human capital. In distinguishing between human capital and human capabilities, for example, Sen (1997) seems to acknowledge that intangible resources (such as human capital) are merely means to capabilities in the relevant sense.

6 It should be noted, however, that an expression of one's agency freedom does not always have to be at odds with one's own interests.

7 See Haq (1996) for an introduction to the human development paradigm (chap. 2) and its influence on the Human Development Reports (chap. 3) and Human Development Index (chap. 4).

8 Note that this may include taking future generations into account.

9 The idea of human development has often been reduced to or equated with either the Human Development Index (HDI) or what has been labeled the human development paradigm. While the HDI and the human development approach are the two most popular uses of the notion of human development, it is by no means clear that the idea of human development can be reduced to either. Thus, in the rest of this book, the terms 'human development' and 'the human development and capability approach/framework' refer merely to the idea that development should, on the one hand, be committed to promote the normatively relevant ends of people and, on the other hand, that these ends must be conceptualized in terms of capabilities and functionings.

10 Do note that I will not be advocating that local stakeholders should be granted exclusive decision-making rights in the context of setting a development agenda. As I argue in section 3.3, my claim will be more moderate.

11 Drinking Coca-Cola should perhaps even be labeled as a negative capability because of its alleged lack of nutritional value and adverse effect on human health, such as caffeine addiction, increased risk of kidney failure, decrease in metabolism, increased risk of obesity and diabetes, and damage to teeth and bones (Hering-Hanit and Gadoth 2003; Hu and Malik 2010; Kristensen et al. 2005; Malik et al. 2010).

12 See also Robeyns (2011) for some considerations related to specifying the capability approach in general along the basic/advanced and capabilities/functionings distinctions.

13 See also Deneulin (2002) and Fleurbaey (2006) for further discussions of paternalism in the capability approach.

14 Interestingly, Sugden (2006, 2008) has criticized the focus on capabilities for promoting a particularly *liberal* view of the good life. See Argenton and Rossi (2013) for a similar criticism. I shall not pursue this discussion here but rather refer to Qizilbash's (2011) response, in which he argues that whether the capability approach is paternalistic in this sense depends entirely on how we specify the particular account of the capability approach.

15 Claassen (2014, 63–8) identifies five instances in which the promotion of functionings is necessary: absence of capacities for voluntary choice, capability training, capability support, capability surrender, and capability participation.

16 Gasper (2005; and Truong 2005, 2008; Koehler et al. 2012) has, for example, argued (a) for human security to have the central role in a development agenda and has even argued that (b) such a focus should lead us beyond human development. I shall not discuss Gasper's two claims in detail here, however. In regard to (a), I shall not take a stance here on the substance of a development agenda; whether or not 'human security' should be included is a question I leave to further specification. Concerning (b), the notion of human security does not mean abandoning the idea that the *kinds of* goals that a development agenda should specify should be conceptualized in terms of capabilities and functionings. Rather, the human security discourse sets out the normative focus for the particular capabilities and functionings of a development agenda. As such, the human security paradigm could be (re) conceptualized as a particular capability theory of development.

17 Although there are notable differences between a sustainable development discourse and the human development and capability approach—especially the former's particular focus on the environment—I shall not discuss here whether they are compatible or not, although most scholars working on this intersection are positive that the two approaches can be mutually reinforcing. For a discussion of commonalities and challenges in this regard, see Crabtree (2013), Crabtree and Tiwari (forthcoming), Lessmann (2011), Lessmann and Rauschmayer (2013), Rauschmayer et al. (2012), and Rauschmayer and Lessmann (2011).

18 Moreover, some capability scholars, such as Holland (2008), have argued that sustainability is best secured by *limiting* some of the capabilities that people can pursue rather than by forcing them to achieve certain functionings. Limiting capabilities would still allow for a wide variety of capabilities and functionings and cannot therefore be reduced to a focus on a specific functioning, such as living a green lifestyle. I shall not discuss the merits of this proposal here other than to note that it may be compatible with the framework that I set out: we could envision a development agenda that also sets out the capabilities and functionings that we should limit.

19 Note that these four characteristics differ from the four essential components of human development, identified by Haq (1996, 16–20), namely equity, sustainability, productivity, and empowerment. Although there are some thematic overlaps between my characteristics and Haq's four, the important thing to stress is that Haq refers to the more specific human development *paradigm*. Because, as I have argued, we do not necessarily need to reduce human development to this more specific paradigm, my characteristics refer to human development in a broader perspective.

20 There is a concern that what this commitment to agency and the commitment to local authority and self-governance means, which I expand upon in the coming chapters, may be in conflict with my claim that we should conceptualize development goals in terms of capabilities and functionings. In short, is it not inconsistent to claim that individuals can choose their own goals while claiming that they should do so in terms of capabilities and functionings? I address this potential tension in section 2.5 and go on to say more about what I mean by local authority in Chapter 3.

21 For a similar argument, see Barcham (2012, 60).

3 A Republican Account of Local Authority in Development

Much of recent development thinking has been underlined by what we may call *a claim to local authority*. The claim to local authority holds that local stakeholders should be granted more authority in matters of their own development. As a political claim, the claim to local authority is essentially a claim to political freedom: it is a claim for local stakeholders to have the freedom to influence the political decision-making involved in setting, adopting, and implementing development policies. In this chapter I shall defend and specify the claim to local political authority in the context of development policy-making. I do so by grounding the claim in republican theory. On a republican conception, political freedom is characterized by the absence of *domination* (Pettit 1997, vii; 1999, 165; 2012, 3; 2016). A person or a group is subject to domination—that is, lacks political freedom—insofar as another person or group has the power to arbitrarily interfere with the choices and actions of that person or group, whether or not that power is invoked.

Accordingly, the republican account that I shall defend in this chapter specifies the claim to local political authority in three regards. First, granting local stakeholders political authority means that development policies cannot legitimately be implemented without having given local stakeholders an adequate voice in the relevant political decision-making process. Second, this means that the political decision-making process should be guided by certain procedural constraints that, third, regulate both public and private exercises of power through a rule of law and socioeconomic policies and laws.

The chapter is structured as follows: In the first section (3.1), I introduce the claim to local authority as a central concept within the development literature. In the second section (3.2), I argue that the claim to local authority can be interpreted as a claim to two distinct kinds of authority, namely political authority and expert authority and address a potential tension with the claims that I made in Chapter 2. In section 3.3 I proceed to specify a republican conception of the claim to local political authority. In particular, I discuss three central concepts of republican theory—(non)domination, arbitrariness, and rules and regulations—in order to bring out the four aspects of a republican conception of local political authority mentioned above.

3.1 A Claim to Local Authority

The formulation of the Millennium Development Goals (MDGs) in 2000, setting out the global development agenda for the following fifteen years, was largely driven by donors and experts (Fukuda-Parr 2012, 13–15; Fukuda-Parr and Hulme 2011). Yet, the world has seen many changes to its political and economic landscape since then. Most importantly, the fact that many developing countries have in the meantime shed their aid-dependency has ushered in a *claim to local authority*.

What is the claim to local authority? What is it a claim to exactly? The claim to local authority, as I shall preliminarily and minimally define it here, is simply the argument that *local stakeholders should be granted more authority in matters of their own development*. Within the development literature, the claim to local authority underlies several different concepts, such as empowerment, ownership, and indigenous knowledge. Although the different concepts specify local authority in different ways and for different reasons, the overarching idea is that local stakeholders should have more control over their own lives. In the following I shortly analyze these three concepts and show how they all employ some version of the claim to local authority.

The first concept that invokes a claim to local authority is *empowerment*. In its essence, empowerment is the idea that an important means to and/or end of development is to enable local individuals and institutions to become actively involved in their own development (rather than merely being recipients or beneficiaries of development aid). The most recent definition of empowerment can be attributed to Drydyk (2013). In responding to two other definitions of empowerment—as means (Narayan-Parker 2002, 14–15; 2005, 16) and as agency (Alkire 2002, 131; Alsop et al. 2006, 10; Crocker 2008, 157; Drydyk 2008, 236; 2013, 251–3)[1]—Drydyk defines empowerment as the absence of coercive power relations. As Drydyk (2013, 255) argues, empowerment is not only concerned with agency but also with *power*:

> Power is sometimes an asymmetry in which the choices that one group *makes* shape or determine the choices that another group *has*, undeterred by the choices that the second group might make. But it can also be a more subtle asymmetry, in which the more powerful group does not need to do or choose anything.

For example, even if law enforcers do not exercise their power, the fact that they have the power to exercise it is often enough to deter citizens from acting against the law. A crucial part of this understanding of empowerment, then, concerns the extent to which an agent is or is not subject to coercion—directly or indirectly—by another agent.

Being safeguarded against abusive exercises of power does not necessarily entail any activity on part of individual agents and groups. Rather, for agents to be empowered in this sense, a society—or any relevant social relation; in our context, the relationship between local agents and external development organizations—needs rules and laws, which regulate the relationships between citizens.

However, we should not dismiss the active role that agents can play in demanding and establishing such rules, laws, and regulations through democratic influence on public policy. That is, citizens may be more or less empowered in terms of the extent to which they can influence public policy that protects their agency (Haq 1996, 20). It is in this sense that empowerment comes close to what we mean by local authority. Empowerment aims to enable local stakeholders to take control of their own lives and of their own development. Because such control depends on external circumstances—especially public policies—empowerment, I contend, implies that the local stakeholders are granted authority when it comes to shaping these external circumstances: it implies that local stakeholders are free from coercion and are actually granted the ability to influence public decision-making processes. Without granting local stakeholders authority, empowering initiatives are essentially scams.

Another concept that invokes a claim to local authority is the idea of *local development ownership*. On an institutional level, the UN, the World Bank and OECD have all recognized the claim to local ownership. For example, the OECD has included the commitment to local ownership in both the Paris Declaration on Aid Effectiveness, the Accra Agenda for Action as well as the Busan Partnership Agreement, which all stress local ownership and participation as central to the development process (Vandemoortele 2012, 11; OECD 2005, 2008, 2011).

The concept of local development ownership is in many ways similar to the concept of empowerment as it aims to represent the extent to which agents are able to control their own lives. As Drydyk (2013, 252) argues, "the core idea [of empowerment] is the degree to which one's activities are one's own, or, so to speak, the 'ownership' of one's activities." Local ownership, Chambers (1995, 203) argues, arises with the move away from a centralized, technocratic approach to development in which ownership is 'pushed down' and 'handed over' to local development actors. Local development ownership in this sense means that not only should locals participate in the design and implementation of the development projects, but also in the identification, monitoring, evaluation, and policy formulation (Chambers 1995, 203). Several scholars, including Alkire (2002), Drydyk (2005), and Wisor (2012, 121–4), have echoed the need for local participation. Alkire (2002, 129–30) defines participation as "the process of discussion, information gathering, implementation, and evaluation by the group(s) directly affected by an activity" and is thus "a method of decision-making in which the participants who are directly affected by an action make the choice." So defined 'participation' is an essential element of the concept of local development ownership because it empowers people to become active participants of development processes rather than their passive recipients.

However, participation is unlikely to have an impact on the local stakeholders' ownership of the development process unless they are, at the same time, granted authority. That is, as Wisor (2012, 124) argues, although such participatory mechanisms are indeed important for ownership, it is unclear how someone can gain ownership merely by having one's voice included if, for example, the ultimate decision-maker is still in a position to ignore them. Hence, the claim to local development ownership relies on a claim to local authority: that local stakeholders be granted authority when participating in the decision-making process. In absence of such authority local stakeholders can hardly be said to actually have ownership.

A third concept, which can be said to instantiate a claim to local authority, is *indigenous knowledge*. The concept of indigenous knowledge holds that local stakeholders—such as indigenous people—embody knowledge about themselves and the society in which they live. This body of knowledge, the proponents of indigenous knowledge hold, effectively makes them authorities in matters of their own lives. As such, the idea of indigenous knowledge builds on an epistemological claim: that indigenous peoples can contribute relevant knowledge, which is valuable or relevant for the design of development initiatives. Sillitoe (1998, 224), for example, points out that "development initiatives that pay attention to local perceptions and ways are more likely to be relevant to people's needs and to generate sustainable interventions."

The epistemic value of indigenous knowledge, meanwhile, has given rise to the normative claim that local stakeholders should be granted more authority in development decision-making. As Watene and Yap (2015, 53) argue, "[i]f we are serious about the contribution of indigenous peoples, then we must also admit that no serious conversation of indigenous perspectives of sustainable development can take place without it." Likewise, Chambers (1995, 1997) argues that we must recognize the reality of local stakeholders as a legitimate input into the process of understanding and solving development issues, while Sillitoe (1998, 225) argues that not doing so constitutes a "[l]ack of respect for others' ways," which "leads to offensive interference in their lives."

To wit, the idea of indigenous knowledge leads to a claim to local authority because its proponents acknowledge local stakeholders as authorities in matters of their own life. Hence, unlike the previous two uses, the claim to local knowledge is an instrumental part of the concept of indigenous knowledge: local stakeholders should be granted decision-making authority because the decisions will thereby be better informed. Conversely, the concepts of empowerment and local ownership make the claim that local authority is intrinsically valuable—that the capacity to decide in matters of one's own life is normatively important in itself and not merely because decisions will thereby be (epistemically) better.

In sum, the claim to local authority underlies at least three concepts—empowerment, local ownership, and indigenous knowledge—within the development literature. So far, I have only given a minimal definition of the claim to local authority. In the next section I proceed to specify the claim to local authority by grounding it in republican theory.

3.2 Political and Expert Authority

What exactly is the claim to local authority a claim to? I have argued that it is a claim for local stakeholders to have legitimate authority to decide on matters of their own development, such as, in our context, how a development agenda is formulated and implemented. Before we proceed to further investigate and normatively ground the claim to local authority, however, we need to take a step back to consider the domain in which it is a claim to authority. That is, what kinds of authority are relevant to decision-making on development policy in general and the setting of a development agenda in particular? In this section, I argue that local stakeholders can put forward the claim to local authority as a claim to two distinct kinds of authority, namely political authority and expert authority, in order to have authority in matters of their own development.

Most obviously, the setting of a development agenda is a political question: it is a claim to have a voice in deliberations that shape, influence, and ultimately decide upon and endorse a development agenda. In this context, the claim to local authority is a claim to *political authority*. Conversely, and by extension, it is a claim to *not* have a development agenda imposed by some higher authority, because it implies that the local stakeholders have at least some authority in these matters.[2]

However, before a development agenda becomes a political issue, it is arguably processed within another domain, namely the domain of expertise.[3] That is, development experts often provide input to the political process.[4] On the one hand, these inputs allow the participants in the political process to make informed decisions. On the other hand, the input of experts can be used to 'check' the arguments and proposed solutions put forth in the political process. In this way, the domain of expertise and who may legitimately be labeled an expert can potentially influence and shape the political process and outcome. We can read the claim to local authority as the claim that local stakeholders have legitimate expertise when it comes to matters of their own development. The claim to local authority, then, can be read not only as the claim to political authority but also to *expert authority*: it is a claim to have legitimate authority not only to decide on or endorse a development agenda (the political issue) but also to influence the input that shapes the agenda (the expertise issue).

In this chapter and the following one, I shall discuss and defend the claim to local authority in both respects. The remainder of this chapter will be dedicated to defending the claim to local political authority by couching it in terms of republican theory. In Chapter 4, I turn to defend the claim as a claim to expert authority.

3.3 Addressing a Potential Tension

Before I continue, however, I first need to address a potential tension within the framework that I propose in this book. The tension is between my answers to the first and second core research questions, namely how the goals of a development agenda should be conceptualized, on the one hand, and, on the other, who should be involved in setting these goals. It may be objected that my defense of the authority of local stakeholders to set a development agenda, which I will be defending in Chapters 3 and 4, is inconsistent with my claim, in Chapter 2, that development is best conceptualized in terms of capabilities and functionings. Insofar as I grant local stakeholders authority in setting a development agenda—selecting the relevant goals—should they not also be granted authority to decide on how to conceptualize the goals? Moreover, what if the local stakeholders, if granted authority, think that development consists not in expanding functionings and capabilities but merely in improving the rule of law and increasing economic capacity building, or in increasing people's preference satisfaction, even if they primarily understand development as the wider accessibility of consumer goods? While I acknowledge that there may indeed be a tension, in the following I shall argue that the worry can be dispelled because the positions that I advance in relation to the two questions are actually more moderate than this objection makes them out to be.

First of all, the claim to local authority that I specify in Chapters 3 and 4 is not that local stakeholders should be granted *full* authority to make decisions on their own development but rather, more moderately, that they should be granted *greater* authority. We could thus imagine a division of authority in which development ethicists have authority in terms of deciding what *kinds* of goals should be included on a development agenda while local stakeholders have authority in terms of deciding which *particular* goals—that is, capabilities and functionings—should be included on the agenda. If so, there is no tension or inconsistency, because the extent of authority granted to local stakeholders may not cover the authority to decide on how to conceptualize development goals.

Granting development ethicists this kind of authority is not a satisfactory response, however. Indeed, I hold the position that we need to grant that local stakeholders should also have authority—although not exclusive authority—in deciding on the answer to the first question. Deciding on what kinds of goals to include on a development agenda should thus be a matter of consultation and deliberation between development experts, such as development ethicists, and local stakeholders. Moreover, granting local stakeholders authority in this way does not necessarily lead to the alleged tension. The reason for this is that the status of my argument in Chapter 1 has not been that development goals *must* be conceptualized in terms of capabilities and functionings. Rather, my claim is that the capability framework provides the *best* conceptualization of human development by capturing and accommodating the diversity of human ends. Hence, my claim is that whoever is responsible for or involved in selecting development goals would do well to conceptualize them in terms of capabilities and functionings.

There is both an empirical and a normative reason to support the claim that local authority is compatible with conceptualizing development goals within the capability framework. Empirically speaking, in Chapter 2 I offered evidence that local stakeholders do conceptualize their own ends in terms of capabilities and functionings. Recall that I concluded that local stakeholders often describe their living standards, well-being, and aspirations in terms of what they are able to do and be. Even when they highlight the importance of resources, they do so as a means to expand their capability sets. When they were seen as preferring what we could call negative or nonvaluable capabilities—such as drinking Coca-Cola—these could be interpreted as proxies for other capabilities, such as socioeconomic status or (lack of) access to clean drinking water. In short, the capability framework does seem to capture what local stakeholders would put on a development agenda given the authority to do so.

Normatively speaking, as Binder and Binder (2016) and Bohman (2012) also argue, adopting the capability framework provides further normative support for the claim that local stakeholders should be granted the freedom to influence the development agenda. As argued in Chapter 2, the capability framework aims to capture the agency aspect of development: the freedom that people have to decide on and pursue their own ends. The claim to local authority is thus complementary to the capability framework because it grants local stakeholders a measure of self-governance (Binder and Binder) or 'communicative power' (Bohman). Conversely, the capability framework also provides a normative and conceptual grounding of the claim to local authority, highlighting the normative importance of local stakeholders' freedom to decide on and pursue their own ends. Therefore, conceptualizing development goals in terms of capabilities and functionings may serve to underscore the claim to local authority.

In sum, although the claim to local authority may indeed be in tension with my claim, in Chapter 2, that we ought to adopt the capability framework to conceptualize development goals, this tension is dispelled as soon as we realize that my claims in Chapters 2–4 are more moderate. First of all, I do not claim that local stakeholders should be granted exclusive authority or that development goals must be conceptualized in terms of capabilities and functionings. I do hold, however, that local stakeholders should have an influence on how development goals are conceptualized. Moreover, there are good reasons why they ought to or would adopt the capability framework in this regard: first, because it provides normative and conceptual support for the claim to local authority and, second, because there is empirical evidence that people actually conceive of their goals and aspirations in terms of doings and beings.[5]

3.4 A Republican Conception of Local Political Authority

What is republicanism? Republicans hold that political freedom "is best understood as a sort of structural relationship that exists between persons or groups, rather than as a contingent event" (Lovett 2014) in which a person or a group may exercise what republicans call *domination* over another person or group of persons (Lovett 2001, 2010, Pettit 1997, 2012; Wartenberg 1990). Domination is characterized by the uncontrolled power to *arbitrarily* interfere with someone else's freedom, regardless of whether that power is actually exercised (Pettit 1997, vii; 1999, 165; 2012, 3; 2016). Thus, domination is not only exercised when the power to interfere is exercised but rather it exists through the ongoing possibility that it could be exercised. For example, a master does not only exercise domination over his slaves when he incarcerates him but also in the mere fact that he could do so if he wishes to without fear of retribution. According to republicans, then (political), freedom can only be brought about through the absence of such domination in the relationships between people: someone is (politically) free, that is, only if she enjoys nondomination.

Based on the republican view of political freedom as nondomination, I proceed in the following to develop and specify a republican conception of local political authority in the context of development. While we may specify the claim to local political authority along several different republican accounts, these accounts can best be specified according to their stance within three central republican debates. Thus, in the following I engage in these three core republican debates in turn in order to specify the particular republican account that we should invoke and, accordingly, how we should characterize the claim to local political authority.

3.4.1 *Conditions for Nondomination*

The first republican debate that is relevant for how we conceptualize our claim to local authority concerns what the conditions for (non) domination are. Domination, Lovett (2001) argues, is essentially a social relationship of a specific kind, namely one in which an agent (or group of agents) A is in a position to wield power over another agent (or group of agents) B. The first condition of domination, then, according to Lovett, is that the social relationship suffers from an *imbalance of power*. The imbalance of power, moreover, manifests itself in the social relationship between agents A and B in such a way that B cannot escape the will of agent A. In other words, B is not in a position to agree or disagree to being dominated by A. Thus, the second condition of domination is that B is to some extent *dependent* on the will of agent A.

Yet, the two first conditions are not sufficient for domination. On most accounts, for example, we would hesitate to claim that the parent-child relationship is a case of domination. Thus, according to Lovett, a further condition is necessary to claim that a social relationship suffers from domination. According to republicans, a parent-child relationship constitutes a case of domination insofar as the children are subject to the unregulated—or arbitrary—will of their parents. The third condition of domination, then, according to Lovett, is the *absence of rules* for the regulation of social relationships.

How can domination be exercised? As Pettit (2012, 37–64) argues, we should distinguish between four kinds of domination: vitiation, invasion, invigilation, and intimidation. While the former two kinds (vitiation and invasion) exercise domination through interference, the latter kinds (invigilation and intimidation) are characterized by exercising domination in the absence of interference.

The first way domination can be exercised is by denying someone the resources that person needs to exercise his or her freedom. Pettit (2012, 43) labels this kind of domination *vitiation*. To illustrate how vitiation works, we can imagine how the government of Brazil may recognize the rights of indigenous Indians to participate in discussions concerning the use of their land. Yet the Indians may not be able to participate in the debates because these discussions take place at the local government seat and the Indians lack the resources to get there in time. In this case, we should say that the Indians' freedom to participate in the debates (and thus exercise influence over their own fate) is vitiated because they lack the precondition for this exercise, namely access to an accessible debate forum. While dominance through vitiation may be objectionable, Pettit (2012, 43–4) argues that we should distinguish between vitiation through negligence and vitiation through *invasion*.

Whereas vitiation through negligence does indeed restrict someone's freedom of choice and action, invasion is the deliberate thwarting of another person's freedom. To illustrate the difference between vitiation and invasion, imagine that the government—aware that the indigenous Indians would object to the government's plan for their land—had placed the debates concerning the land use at the seat of the local government exactly because they knew that the indigenous population had no way of getting there in time or that they outright banned the Indians from participating. Because domination through invasion deliberately interferes with the Indians' freedom to influence their own future, we should say that invasion is more objectionable than vitiation.

Vitiation and invasion, however, are not the only ways to exercise domination. Republican theorists hold that domination can be exercised even in the absence of interference. I may, on the one hand, be free in the presence of interference insofar as this interference does not vitiate or invade my freedom to choose or act. In fact, interference may even be necessary for freedom insofar as it seeks to supply someone with the necessary means for exercising his or her freedom. On the other hand, I may be free in the presence of interference insofar as I am in control of the interference. Thus, Pettit (2012, 56–9) concludes, interference is neither necessary nor sufficient for domination. As a consequence we should identify two further kinds of domination, namely invigilation and intimidation (Pettit 2012, 60–4). While the two may be present at the same time, they can also be exercised apart: invigilation can be exercised without intimidation and vice versa.

Invigilation is the idea that someone has the power to interfere with the freedom of someone else, whether or not that power is exercised. Imagine that the indigenous Indians were given the opportunity to determine the use of their land but that the Brazilian government still retained the right to override the Indians' decision should it so wish to. In this example, the Brazilian government subjects the indigenous Indians to domination because they invigilate their choices.

Intimidation is the idea that someone is believed to have the power to interfere with the choices of someone else, even if that person or group in fact does not possess this power. Imagine, for example, that the Brazilian government had ratified a hypothetical international convention delegating the land rights to the indigenous Indians. In this case, the government does not actually have the power to invigilate (or interfere with) the choices of the Indians. Yet, the Indians may themselves be unaware of this fact and thus believe that the government can interfere with their choice if it so wishes to. As a result, they may be more disposed to make choices, which they suspect the Brazilian government would be less likely to interfere with. In this way, we should say that the Brazilian government holds dominance over the Indians insofar as it is able to intimidate them with the effect of coercing them to make certain choices.

Because all four kinds of domination have the potential to influence the freedom of the local stakeholders to set a development agenda, we should insist that our conception of local political authority should be sensitive to these ways of exercising power. Let us accordingly specify the claim to local political authority in the following way:

> *Specification #1*: Local political authority should be defined as the absence of external domination and thus, in order to be present,

> demands that all four kinds of domination—vitiation, invasion, invigilation, and intimidation—are absent or regulated.

That is not to say that our conception of local political authority should prohibit all involvement of external development agents in the process of setting a development agenda. Rather, it means that insofar as external stakeholders usually have more power than the local stakeholders, the relationship between external and local stakeholders is vulnerable to the arbitrary exercise of power in the four ways mentioned. This raises two questions, which will be analyzed in the following two subsections. First, when exactly does the exercise of power instantiate a case of domination? That is, how should we define the notion of *arbitrary* power (section 2.2)? Second, how can our conception of local political authority avoid that imbalanced or asymmetric relationships between external and local stakeholders become vulnerable to the exercise of domination? That is, what measures should we take to regulate this relationship, ensuring that local political authority is robust and not subject to domination (section 2.3)?

3.4.2 *Substantive and Procedural Definitions of Arbitrariness*

The second republican debate that we need to consider concerns how to define 'arbitrariness.' Recall that republicans understand domination as the power to *arbitrarily* interfere with the choices and actions of others (Lovett 2012, 137; Lovett and Pettit 2009, 14; Costa 2007, 291; List 2006, 201).[6] There are two ways of defining arbitrary power within republican theory, namely procedurally and substantively (Lovett 2015, 2012). On the *substantive* definition, the exercise of power is arbitrary insofar as it fails to track the interests or preferences of those affected by its exercise (Pettit 1997, 55–6; List 2006, 202) while on the *procedural* view, it is arbitrary insofar as it is not reliably constrained by a rule of law (Lovett 2012, 139–40; List 2006, 202). Now, what definition of 'arbitrariness' should our republican conception of local political authority adopt?

The first thing we should notice is that the claim made by our republican conception of local political authority is weaker or stronger according to whether it adopts a substantive or procedural definition of arbitrariness. On the one hand, adopting a procedural definition makes a weaker claim insofar as it only demands that the procedure, by which a development agenda is formulated, respects certain procedural constraints (Lovett 2012, 139–40; List 2006, 202). Adopting a substantive definition, on the other hand, arguably places a stronger demand on development policy than the procedural definition. According to the substantive definition, a development agenda must be adequately representative of the preferences and interests of local stakeholders, whether expressed through a deliberative democratic exercise or manifested in a recognized fund of social norms (Lovett 2012, 144; Skinner 1998, 26; Pettit 2004). Hence, on the substantive definition, it is not only necessary that local stakeholders have had the opportunity to contest the agenda, but also that the agenda itself represent their expressed interests and preferences.

There are two reasons for us to adopt this stronger, substantive definition when applied to the setting of a development agenda. First, a development agenda contains substantive goals that represent the development of the local stakeholders. Thus, it can be argued, whether or not our development agenda constitutes a case of domination depends at least partially on the extent to which it is substantively representative in this way. If this is true, then the weaker, procedural definition is unsuitable because it does not ensure that the agenda is substantively representative of the local stakeholders' interests, preferences, or shared norms.

However, proponents of the procedural definition may object, it is not sufficient that the agenda is substantively justified. That is, they could argue, local political authority is also concerned with the extent to which the political procedure of setting a development agenda includes local stakeholders and respects their input. Even if an agenda were substantively representative, it would still violate the claim to local political authority insofar as local stakeholders had insufficient opportunity to participate in the procedure of formulating and adopting the agenda. If so, we should rather adopt the procedural definition.

The second reason for adopting the substantive, deliberative definition is that this procedural objection does not have any bite because the substantive definition includes the procedural definition (Lovett 2012, 143). That is, we can only arrive at a substantively representative development agenda insofar as there is a reliable procedure in place to track the local stakeholders' expressed interests, preferences, or shared norms. As such, it is possible to dispel the main reason for opting for a procedural definition, namely that a suitable development policy requires a procedural justification, because such a justification is also provided by the substantive definition (Rawls 1999, 74). In other words, on the substantive definition, the process of setting a development agenda is just insofar as it can ensure that the procedure arrives at a just outcome (i.e., an agenda, which is substantively representative).

Yet, we should ask whether this substantive definition is not too demanding. I believe it is. The changing contexts of development—not only in terms of sociocultural and environmental circumstances but also as a matter of changes over time—should lead us to leave the outcome of the process open-ended. As such, what we want from development policy is not primarily to represent the preferences and norms of local stakeholders. Rather, we want development policy to be critical of unjust socioeconomic norms that hold back local development processes; we want the policies to not only represent local norms and preferences but also more technical solutions or normative insights. We want a development agenda to integrate these different aspects.

Thus, a definition of the claim to local political authority, which holds that development policy must be substantively representative of local norms, is too strong because it aims to transfer all authority from external to local stakeholders. Such a full transfer of authority is counterproductive to development because a sustainable approach to development requires the input of external stakeholders *in addition to* being representative of local stakeholders. For these reasons I propose that the republican claim to local political authority adopts the procedural definition.[7] On a procedural definition, the process of development policy-making is respectful of the claim to local political authority insofar as it adheres to certain procedural constraints. Let us therefore define the second specification of the claim to local authority in the following way:

> *Specification #2*: Local political authority demands that development policy is formulated, adopted, and implemented according to a political process, which respects certain procedural constraints.

Now, what kinds of constraints should a procedure for development policy-making adhere to? In the following subsection, I argue that a third republican debate—on the scope of accountability—can help us specify these constraints further.

3.4.3 Rules, Regulations, and Public Policies

In the previous two subsections I argued that we can specify the claim to local political authority in two ways. First, I argued that local political authority should be defined as the absence of four kinds of domination, namely vitiation, invasion, invigilation, and intimidation. Any of these four kinds of domination allows for the arbitrary exercise of power. Second, I argued that local political authority merely requires that certain procedural constraints are respected. That is, a development agenda satisfies the claim to local political authority insofar as the procedure of formulating, adopting, and implementing the agenda adheres to certain constraints and regulations.

This prompts us to ask the question: what kinds of constraints and regulations should the procedure adhere to? Republicans usually look to curb the arbitrary use of power through the implementation of a set of rules, regulations, and public policies. In the following, I first explain why republican theory needs a set of rules and regulations before I turn to outline the kinds of institutions and public policies, which republicans favor and that can help us specify the claim to local authority further.

On a republican account, the prospect of local political authority in the context of development policy-making faces two threats, which Pettit (2006, 279) refers to as *public* and *private* instances of domination, respectively.[8] Publicly, local stakeholders are vulnerable to the expert-rule of international development organizations as well as from corrupt or dysfunctional national governments. Securing local political authority thus requires the regulation of the relationship between the local stakeholders and development policy-makers. At the same time, local political authority also faces dangers related to private domination, although this may be less obvious from what has been said so far. To see how, we need merely consider the danger that a select few locals take control of the decision-making process, ignoring the values and preferences of their fellow citizens and passing off their own worldview as representative of society in general. Accordingly, the outcome of the process would favor these select few agents.

What kinds of institutions and public policies are needed to ensure that the arbitrary exercise of power is curbed? To begin with, we should note that addressing the two kinds of domination—public and private—requires two different strategies (Pettit 2006, 279–80): while curbing public domination requires regulation with regard to how a governing body can interfere with its subjects, private domination is best addressed by policies that secure the equal status of citizens so no one is in a position to impose his or her power on others. In other words, the public exercise of power is nonarbitrary insofar as it is somehow regulated by a rule of law, while a private exercise of power is rendered nonarbitrary insofar as it respects the other person as an equal agent.[9] Let us take a look at some of the concrete suggestions republicans have proposed to keep public and private domination in check.

As I have argued in the previous subsections, securing local political authority primarily requires procedural or democratic regulations. To wit, in a public context, the claim to local political authority demands that external stakeholders and national governments are answerable to some sort of democratic rule when setting a development agenda. A robust democratic rule must satisfy three conditions (cf. Pettit 1997, chap. 6). First, decision-makers must be able to provide reasons for their decisions, which are open to public debate. Second, everyone should have an equal opportunity for democratic contestation. Third, there should be democratic institutions, which facilitate the process of public contestation.

I believe these conditions are essential for the claim to local political authority too. What do the conditions specifically mean for local stakeholders? Most obviously, in order to satisfy these conditions, we need to ensure that local stakeholders have the capability—that is, real freedom—to vote, to participate in public discussions, and to contest the decisions of the governing body (Maynor 2003, 2006, Pettit 1997, 2006). Moreover, for local stakeholders to have such capabilities, they need equal access to public institutions that are transparent and fair.[10] Yet regulating the relationship between local stakeholders and more powerful development agents, such as national governments and international development organizations, is only part of ensuring that local political authority is robust. Differences in socioeconomic conditions between local stakeholders may also cause political authority to be unequally distributed between stakeholders. Some scholars, for example, have argued that there is a correlation between economic wealth and political power, effectively leading to a state of plutocracy: the domination of a wealthy elite (Christiano 2010, 2012).

How can we avoid differences in socioeconomic power leading to such cases of private domination? In order to support the claim to local political authority, we can invoke two means. First, we may enact *public policies* in a bid to level the socioeconomic playing field between individuals. Because people who are socioeconomically disadvantaged are vulnerable to exploitation by or dependent on more resourceful people (Dagger 2006, Lovett 2009, 2010), public policies may serve to minimize the risk of domination. Employees who depend on their income to meet basic needs are, arguably, less likely to object to poor working conditions—for example by endorsing a progressive development agenda—if it means that they will lose their employment status and precious income. Providing socioeconomically disadvantaged people with basic goods and capabilities reduces this risk of exploitation and dependence and thus promotes their political freedom. That is, the workers may feel more confident in speaking out against their poor working conditions when debating a development agenda if they are able to meet their basic needs independently of an income from their labor.

Second, republicans aim to curb such private cases of domination, which impact people's political freedom, by invoking *public laws*. That is, by enshrining citizens' rights to, for example, decent working conditions, a minimum wage, or basic living standards into the law they will be less vulnerable to exploitation. In keeping with the aforementioned case, laws protecting workers' rights, for example, curb the power an employer can exercise over her employees without fear of punishment. As such, public laws play an important role in regulating private relations and minimize the risk of some citizens (e.g., employers) influencing the voice of other citizens (e.g., employees) in general and in particular in relation to the political process of setting a development agenda.[11]

Ensuring that local stakeholders have political authority in the context of setting a development agenda requires that they are not subject to domination, defined as the power of one (group of) individual(s) to arbitrarily impose their power over another (group of) individual(s). In this subsection, I have argued that the claim to local political authority faces threats from both public and private exercises of arbitrary power. I have argued that in order to protect local political authority, we should adopt the republican notion of a rule of law, which can regulate both public and private exercises of power. Let us therefore define the third specification of the claim to local authority in the following way:

> *Specification #3*: Local political authority should be protected by a rule of law in order to procedurally regulate both public and private exercises of power, including democratic rights, public laws, and public policies.

In sum, in this section I have argued that we can and should specify the claim to local political authority in three ways with the help of republican theory. First, the claim to local political authority should be understood as the claim that local stakeholders should not be subject to domination—from national policy-makers or external development experts—in the political process of setting a development agenda. Second, I have argued that the claim to local political authority should be understood as a procedural claim. As a procedural claim, the claim to local political authority holds that the political process of setting a development agenda should respect certain procedural constraints that restrict the extent to which power can be exercised. Third, I have argued that local political authority is threatened by both public and private exercises of power. Publicly, policy-makers and external development experts and stakeholders may overrule local stakeholders; privately, socioeconomic inequalities make weaker parties vulnerable to exploitation by more resourceful and powerful citizens.

3.4.4 *Positive or Negative Freedom?*

Republicans usually argue that the concept of nondomination is distinct from the traditional conceptualization of political freedom as either negative or positive. However, as I will argue in the following, republicans would do well to adopt aspects of both positive and negative freedom in order to (a) include a comprehensive view of political freedom and (b) bring it more in line with the notion of real or substantive freedom within the capability approach.

According to Berlin (1969), we can distinguish between two conceptualizations of freedom. On the negative conception, freedom is characterized by the absence of interference. Someone is free insofar as no one or nothing interferes with or impedes with his choice to perform a certain action. Accordingly, republicans often refer to the negative conception of freedom as *freedom as noninterference*. For example, as Lovett (2014, sec. 1.1) argues, all conceptions of negative freedom "have in common the basic intuition that to be free is, more or less, to be left alone to do whatever one chooses." In the context of development, a negative conception of political freedom would hold that local stakeholders are politically free insofar as they can exercise their democratic rights, including expressing their opinions, participating in public debates, and voting in elections and referenda, without anyone interfering with that choice (Steiner 1994).

In comparison, on Berlin's conception of positive freedom, freedom is characterized by the internal capacity to rationally exercise control over one's choice, rather than to be swayed by one's unreflected desires.[12] To illustrate, the smoker who knows that smoking is unhealthy yet continues to smoke is not free on the positive conception of freedom. Rather, only by overriding her desire to smoke does she exercise her positive freedom. Accordingly, positive political freedom is usually equated with self-determination: "one might say that a democratic society is a free society because it is a self-determined society, and that a member of that society is free to the extent that he or she participates in its democratic process" (Carter 2012, sec. 1). In the present context, then, we should say that local stakeholders have positive political freedom insofar as they exercise their self-determination by participating in the decision-making on what kind of development goals that should apply to their society.

Republicans hold that both the negative and positive conceptions of freedom are inadequate at capturing the notion of (non)domination. Negative freedom on Berlin's conception, republicans argue, is inadequate for two reasons. First of all, it does not protect local stakeholders against domination through invigilation and intimidation (Lovett 2014). Even if no one interferes with the authority of local stakeholders, their freedom to exercise this authority might still depend on the contingent and arbitrary willingness of, for example, international development organizations to grant them this authority. Second, the notion of freedom as noninterference does not take account of the fact that it is often necessary to interfere with some people's freedom in order to ensure freedom for everyone. Consider, for example, how a few individuals might control the political direction of a local community, suppressing the voices of less powerful individuals. In this case, it might be necessary to interfere, externally, with the self-determination of the community at large in order to secure the political freedom of these marginalized individuals.

Positive freedom, according to republicans, is inadequate to capture the notion of nondomination because it may actually justify interfering with people's choices (Lovett and Pettit 2009, 15). The problem is that because Berlin's conception of positive freedom can only be exercised through rational and reflected choices, it justifies interfering with irrationally motivated choices and actions. Thus, if the choices and decisions of the local stakeholders are somehow deemed to be based on irrational beliefs, this positive conception of freedom provides justification for interfering with these decisions. As Taylor (1985, 216) argues, however, Berlin's positive conception of freedom relies on a questionable (metaphysical or psychological) view of rationality in which desires can directly be controlled by reason. If no such control of reason over desire can be exercised, then the distinction between rational and irrational choices and decisions is difficult to sustain. Consequently, according to republicans, interfering with a local community because their decisions are deemed to be irrational would be arbitrary and constitute a case of domination.

However, the problem is that proponents of both negative and positive freedom can argue that they hold stronger views of freedom than represented by Berlin's conceptions. Consequently, in both cases republicans argue against a straw man by distinguishing the republican concept of freedom as nondomination in opposition to Berlin's conceptions of negative and positive freedom.

According to proponents of negative freedom, republicans mischaracterize negative freedom in two ways. First of all, negative freedom does not entail that infringements on freedom are always unjustified—indeed, they may be quite common and unavoidable, for example as part of a social contract (Hobbes 1991, chaps. 14 and 21; Steiner 1994). Rather, proponents of negative freedom only hold that infringements on freedom can only be justified with the express consent of the subject. As such, some interference with the freedom of local stakeholders can be justified insofar as the communities themselves sanction them. Second, proponents of negative freedom do acknowledge that a comprehensive conception of political freedom requires that some positive conditions are fulfilled (Sen 1988, 273; Knight 1982, 15), such as access to democratic institutions, but that political freedom cannot be reduced to these positive conditions: some negative freedom is still necessary in order for people to be able to freely take advantage of these positive conditions. Consider, again, how someone may have access to a polling station—a positive condition—yet not be free to vote insofar as she is restricted from voting.

A republican conception of local authority can and should conditionally accept these two amendments to negative freedom. First of all, consent is a central aspect of republican freedom. As argued, an asymmetric power relationship can only be justified on the republican view insofar as the disadvantaged party can freely consent to it. However, republicans further hold that such an asymmetric relationship still needs to be regulated in order to prevent the more powerful part from dominating the less powerful part, for example through exploitation and intimidation. Second, republicans, like proponents of negative freedom, hold that noninterference is necessary for nondomination. However, according to republicans, local political authority can only partially be covered by negative freedom. The exercise of someone's negative freedom still partly depends on whether they possess the positive means to do so. Whether the indigenous Brazilians in our earlier example can exercise their right to participate in the debate on the use of their land depends on whether they have the means to get to the venue where the debate is held as well as the oral skills to make their case in a convincing manner.

Like the proponents of negative freedom, the proponents of positive freedom could rightly object that republicans object to a limited view of positive freedom. Again, this is in two regards. First of all, Taylor (1985) argues, positive freedom does not necessarily justify paternalistic interventions with choices and decisions that are deemed irrational. According to Taylor (1985, 228–9) positive freedom is not the exercise of one's rational capacities but rather constituted by a phenomenological or hermeneutical self-understanding through which we exercise our freedom by making *strong evaluations*:

> We experience our desires and purposes as qualitatively discriminated, as higher or lower, noble or base, integrated or fragmented, significant or trivial, good and bad. This means that we experience some of our desires and goals as intrinsically more significant than others.

Positive freedom, on this view, is exercised when we distinguish those desires that are important to being our distinct selves (Taylor 1985, 218). For example, I might find practicing my religion as constitutive of myself and thus more important than the desire to cross the street without stopping for the red light.

Second, the notion that positive freedom is exercised through making strong evaluations highlights the fact that freedom requires certain positive conditions to be satisfied. According to Taylor (1991), because we are not merely atomistic individuals, our identities, values, and choices are (partly) shaped against a backdrop of social norms and institutions. Hence, in order to exercise their positive freedom—that is, in order to make strong evaluations about their own self-understanding—it is necessary to ensure that they have access to these identity-forming institutional and social environments. On Taylor's account, then, positive political freedom can only be exercised insofar as this social and insitutional background that allow individuals and communities to participate in the collective self-determination, for example through public deliberation, is provided.[13]

Again, republicans can and should conditionally accept these two aspects of positive freedom as part of a republican conception of local political authority. First of all, the emphasis on strong evaluations is a central aspect of local political authority. As Larmore (2001, 232) argues, it is "plain that Pettit's theory of freedom as non-domination, distinct though it is from the 'positive' conception of freedom as autonomy, accords nonetheless an essential role to democratic self-rule" (see also Pettit 1997, 8, 183ff). That is, local stakeholders can avoid being dominated by other stakeholders' interests by exercising their capacity for self-determination, for example through a deliberation on a development agenda.

Second, a republican conception of local political authority should accommodate that, as Sen (1988) and Knight (1982) have argued, a comprehensive account of political freedom certain positive conditions to be satisfied. Conversely, this also means that domination can be exercised by denying these positive conditions. In order for local stakeholders to be able to exercise their political freedom in the context of setting a development agenda, they need at least access to the relevant debate—for example, through researchers or open hearings—and the ability to adequately express their preferences and objections, which requires a minimum level of education.

Although a republican conception of local political authority can accommodate both aspects of positive freedom, republicans should still insist that a comprehensive conception of local political authority must go beyond positive freedom. First of all, Taylor's concept of positive freedom is still vulnerable to the exercise of domination because it requires that individual members of a community adhere, to a certain extent, to the social norms of the community. This leaves less room for individual dissent to the social norms among oppressed, disadvantaged, and marginalized members of society, such as in the case of the Indian caste system (Walzer 1983, 313). Second, as in the case of negative freedom, local political authority cannot be reduced to the presence of certain positive conditions that allow people to exercise this freedom. As argued, even if one has access to the polling station, one still needs the negative freedom to not be interfered with in order to exercise one's freedom to vote.[14]

Thus, in sum, a republican conception of political freedom and local political authority should integrate aspects of both negative and positive freedom. As such, we can further specify our republican conception of local political authority in the following way:

> *Specification #4*: The claim to local political authority requires that both negative and positive aspects of political freedom are met.

The benefits of integrating aspects of negative and positive freedom are twofold. First, it provides a more comprehensive account of freedom, which recognizes that domination can be exercised by denying both the negative and positive preconditions for exercising freedom. Second, by integrating negative and positive aspects of political freedom, a republican conception of local political authority has the added benefit that it satisfies the idea of real freedom proposed by Sen (1988) that is central to the human development and capability approach.[15] As such, on this conception of local political authority, the political freedom of local stakeholders is not merely a formal opportunity but a substantive one, which local stakeholders may choose to realize (or not).

3.5 Concluding Remarks

In this chapter, I have specified the claim to local authority in the political context of setting a development agenda. Recall that the claim to local authority is the claim that local stakeholders should be granted both political and expert authority in relation to the task of setting a development agenda. Politically speaking, I have argued that the claim to local authority should draw on republican theory. I have labeled this *a republican conception of local political authority.*

In particular, republican theory can help us specify local political authority in at least four ways. First, the claim to local political authority should be understood as the claim that local stakeholders should not be subject to domination, understood as the arbitrary exercise of power, in the political process of setting a development agenda, from national policy-makers, external stakeholders, or fellow citizens. Second, the claim to local political authority holds that the political process of setting a development agenda should respect certain procedural constraints that restrict the extent to which power can be exercised, *not* that the development agenda must substantively represent the preferences and values of the local stakeholders. Third, I have argued that local political authority is threatened by both public and private exercises of power, the regulation of which requires different strategies, such as a rule of law and public socioeconomic policies and laws. Finally, a republican conception of local political authority should adopt aspects of both negative and positive freedom.

Ensuring that local stakeholders enjoy political authority, however, is only part of the claim to local authority in the context of setting a development agenda. As I argued in the previous chapter, a development agenda is also shaped by the advice from different experts. In the next chapter, I shall argue that local stakeholders can legitimately be considered experts in relation to their own development and that consequently they should be granted what I call *local expert authority.*

Notes

1 I shall not discuss these alternative definitions of empowerment here but rather refer to the discussion in Drydyk (2013).
2 Note that this does not exclude the idea that we, in practice, need to hand over some authority in order to enforce policy. Rather, this is consistent with the idea behind democracy: that citizens are the owners of the policy and the law because they are the authors of it through democratic participation.
3 We should condition this sentence in two ways. First of all, I do not mean to imply here that the process of soliciting expert advice necessarily comes chronologically before the political process. The process of expert advice might proceed simultaneously with the political process. Second, although the process of expert advice is distinct here from the political process, I do not mean to imply that it is not tainted by political discussions. In fact, as we shall

see in Chapter 4, the political process often has a bearing on the conclusions of experts. Nonetheless, I insist that we should keep the two domains apart because, as I argue, we can distinguish the claim to local authority, at least analytically, differently whether it is put forth as a claim to political or expert authority.

4 I take a broad view of development expertise here to include earth sciences and social sciences, as well as the humanities (ethics and rhetorical studies come to mind as especially relevant).

5 We can derive three conclusions from this: while (1) my answer to the second question is analytically independent from my answer to the first question and (2) my answer to the third question requires that we adopt my answer to the first question, (3) my answer to the second question is consistent with and in support of the answers I provide to both the first and the third questions and vice versa.

6 As argued, the power to interfere does not in itself constitute domination. This is so in two ways. First, interference can sometimes be necessary in order to expand political freedom. As an example, the international community may interfere with a state's power to subject its citizens to its will, thus expanding the political freedom of the citizens. Moreover, a government may, for example, impose certain taxes on its citizens – thus interfering with their economic capability – in order to finance public goods, such as education and health care, which expands the freedom of the citizens. Second, the power to interfere does not constitute domination insofar as the people who are subject to it somehow sanction it. Consider, for example, how the citizens of (representative) democracies delegate the power to implement laws and policies to a select few politicians and lawmakers. Now, on the republican conception, what distinguishes domination from legitimate interference is that, in cases of domination, and to stay with our example, lawmakers and policy-makers have the ability to implement laws and policies on an arbitrary basis.

7 I should stress that I do not claim here that the procedural definition is preferable in all contexts in which we apply republican theory. My claim is merely that *in the specific context of development policy-making* the procedural definition is preferable to the substantive definition because it (a) does not entail a full transfer of authority and (b) leaves the outcome of the process open-ended.

8 In other places Pettit (1997, chaps. 5–6) uses the terms 'imperium' and 'dominium' – which he adopts from Kriegel (1995) – for the two kinds of domination (see also McMahon 2005, 68). I shall here prefer the public/private terminology, as it is more indicative of the respective spaces of domination.

9 For a similar view on the difference between the rights and duties of the governing body vis-à-vis its subjects and the rights and duties owed to other citizens; see, for example, Weintraub and Kumar (1997, 10–16).

10 Note that these requirements are only suggestions. As with a development agenda, the democratic rights and institutions should be tailored to the specific society. I have provided a similar argument elsewhere against the view that we can specify a particular list of (democratic) capabilities through mere normative political theorizing (Byskov 2017a).

11 Republicans recognize, however, that no matter what, domination will always pose a threat to political freedom (Pettit 2006, 282–3; Lovett 2015). See Pettit (2006, 282–3) for a discussion of three issues, which he refers to as the problems of the imperfect, the ineffective, and the unauthorized state.

12 See also Frankfurt (1971)

13 See also Sen (1988) and Knight (1982) for a similar conclusion.

14 We should note that this is not necessarily incompatible with the positive conception of freedom. What positive freedom holds may merely be interpreted as the claim that some positive measure of freedom is necessary for a full conception of freedom.

15 For a similar view of freedom to that of Sen (and other capability theorists), see also MacCallum's (1967) *triadic* conception of freedom. Freedom, MacCallum argues, is a triadic relation that captures the extent to which (1) an agent is constrained by (2) certain conditions in relation to (3) certain things that he can do or be(come). Positive and negative freedom, MacCallum argues, are merely two different interpretations of this triadic relationship, which hold different assumptions about what an agent is, what a constricting condition is (e.g., internal or external), and what counts as something that one can strive to do or be. Regardless of how the proponents of positive and negative freedom specify this triadic relationship, it will contain both positive and negative aspects because it involves both the freedom *from* something and the freedom *to do or be(come)* something. Thus, MacCallum argues that the dichotomy between positive and negative freedom is false.

4 Third Wave Development Expertise

While a development agenda may receive its final endorsement and adoption at the political level, which I addressed in the previous chapter, an important step leading up to this adoption occurs at a different level, namely the socioscientific one. Although development experts, working for international development organizations, have traditionally spearheaded development efforts at the socioscientific level, this top-down, technocratic approach has recently been challenged. Several scholars have argued that development experts often get local socioeconomic dynamics wrong (e.g., Ferguson 1990, 1994; Keene 2007; World Bank 1994), while other scholars stress that the insights, knowledge, and perspectives of local stakeholders can make significant contributions to our understanding of development (e.g., Briggs 2005; Sillitoe 2004; Watene and Yap 2015). These challenges invite us to ask: What is 'development expertise'? What counts as legitimate expert knowledge, and who can legitimately claim to be experts? Given the authority that experts have in influencing development policy, it becomes crucial to determine who can claim such expert authority and on the basis of what kind of knowledge.

In this chapter I offer a normative account of development expertise. Although extending expertise beyond the traditional development experts to include local stakeholders, this normative account aims to delimit legitimate forms of expertise based on Collins and Evans's (2002, 2008) taxonomy of expert knowledge. I label this normative view *third wave development expertise*.[1] This label aims to distinguish this normative view of development expertise from the traditional technocratic view of expertise (first wave development expertise) as well as the social constructivist view of development expertise embodied by proponents of indigenous knowledge (second wave development expertise).

In particular, I discuss Collins and Evans's notions of *contributory* and *interactional* expertise. Contributory expertise denotes the extent to which an agent or group of agents possesses (tacit, embodied, or explicit) knowledge which can make a significant contribution to a particular scientific area (e.g., Wynne 1989)—in this case, development—while interactional expertise denotes the extent to which they are able to communicate this knowledge meaningfully. I note that while local stakeholders may possess (tacit) contributory expertise in matters of their own development, they may lack interactional expertise to make a contribution to wider debates about development. Conversely, some may possess interactional expertise—that is, be able to 'talk the talk'—yet lack any real understanding of the subject matter.

I argue that third wave development expertise contributes to the development literature in two novel ways.[2] First, it establishes that there are clearly some forms of knowledge which do not count as legitimate contributory development expertise and why. Second, I argue that where local stakeholders may be said to have contributory expertise, yet lack interactional expertise, their tacit knowledge needs to be articulated by someone who does possess adequate interactional expertise, or the local stakeholders must improve their ability to communicate scientifically. Likewise, development experts who possess substantial knowledge about development must acquire the interactional expertise necessary, or employ a translator to communicate properly with local stakeholders. This, I argue, may call for a mediator who can interact with and between external experts and local stakeholders.

The chapter is structured as follows: In Section 4.1 I explain the move from first to second wave (development) expertise. In Section 4.2 I present and discuss Collins and Evans's notion of third wave expertise, with a particular emphasis on what they call contributory and interactional forms of expertise. Section 4.3 applies the notion of third wave expertise to the domain of development. In particular, I argue that we should adopt a third wave view of development expertise, which includes embodied and tacit knowledge. In Section 4.4 I argue that we can identify five types of experts to mediate between technical development experts and local stakeholders. In Section 4.5 I address three objections to the third wave view of development expertise.

4.1 Positivism, Social Constructivism, and Development Expertise

Development can be characterized as a socioscientific issue. A socioscientific issue is a social issue which has a conceptual or technological link to science or, conversely, a scientific issue which has a clear social impact (Sadler 2004). Like issues related to stem cell research, nuclear energy, and global warming, how to achieve development poses a "complex, open-ended, often contentious" dilemma (Sadler 2004, 514) which the public has an interest in solving because of its impact on how we live (Bingle and Gaskell 1994, 186).

Solving socioscientific issues such as development involves a strong scientific component, which relies on input from the scientific community. Within development, we may conceive of this scientific input quite broadly to include, among others, economics, ethics, sociology, epidemiology, agricultural science, water management, anthropology, and more recently, the Earth sciences and philosophy of technology.

Making judgments about socioscientific issues often requires information which is "complex, arising from multiple sources, and is often inconclusive" (Bingle and Gaskell 1994, 186). Consequently, decision-making about socioscientific issues is often disputed and contentious (Bingle and Gaskell 1994, 186). Development policy is no different. This complexity raises questions about who can legitimately contribute to providing such input. In other words, who can legitimately claim authority as development experts? What counts as legitimate expert knowledge? In this section I discuss two views of (development) expertise, namely the positivist and the social constructivist, and argue that they are both inadequate as notions of development expertise.

4.1.1 The First Wave of Development Expertise: A Positivist View

From a *positivist* view, scientific knowledge derives from the formal processes of deduction and induction (Sadler 2004, 514) and can be distinguished from other forms of knowledge because of its formal structure which adheres to specific scientific norms (Bingle and Gaskell 1994, 190; Longino 1983, 7; Sadler 2004, 514), such as the Mertonian principles (Macfarlane and Cheng 2008; Merton 1973).[3] According to the positivist view, legitimate scientific claims must undergo rigorous testing following these principles and is only validated when the scientific community has been able to replicate and confirm the claims (Bingle and Gaskell 1994, 190; Cole 1992, 6).

Science is considered value-free in the positivist view. This means, as Longino (1983, 7) explains, "that scientific practice ought to be independent of personal, social, and cultural values and that the practice of scientists as scientists is independent of their subjective preferences regarding what ought to be." Although this makes the scientific discussion open to anyone in principle (Bingle and Gaskell 1994, 190), scientific expertise is in practice esoteric[4] within the positivist view because "the public has no practical access to the standards used by scientists to judge good and bad science" without scientific literacy, that is, "the same level of education and practical experience as a professional scientist" (Bingle and Gaskell 1994, 193).

Traditional approaches to development clearly embody the positivist view on development expertise—if not explicitly then at least implicitly; if not by design then at least by default—in which "the privileged status of the technical expert" took hold in Western societies' ideal of decision-making in the late nineteenth century (Brand and Karvonen 2007, 22; see also Hickman 1992; Seely 1996). As Western leaders turned their attention toward the development of the Third World they naturally adopted the positivist, technocratic approach (Bucchi 2009, 2–3; Cooke 2003, 2004; Wilson 2006, 504). This tradition was further carried over into the work of inter-governmental and international development organizations.

Since the mid-1980s, however, the positivist view has been under scrutiny with critics arguing that (socio)scientific reasoning and decision-making neither can nor should be considered independently of social values and contexts. We can identify two general sets of critiques aimed at the positivist position.

The first set of critiques aims to show how scientific reasoning and consensus in fact rely on value statements and social contexts, such as power, biases, influences, and strategic interests. Consequently, scientific reasoning cannot be seen independently from its social context, which puts into question the *boundary* between scientific and nonscientific reasoning as well as between expert and nonexpert authority. While one of the hallmarks of the positivist position is the claim that scientific reasoning and consensus is fundamentally different from other forms of reasoning because of its formal structure, sociologists of science argue that scientific reasoning and consensus is more similar to public reasoning and decision-making than proponents of positivism have claimed.

According to this criticism, scientists are just as prone as the public to be influenced by values and social contexts (Bingle and Gaskell 1994, 191; Longino 1983, 8). In her analysis of socioscientific practice, Longino (1983, 13), for example, concludes that "non-epistemological, personal, social, or cultural values have affected scientific practice," both externally, for example through allocation of research funds or general trends in areas of research (Longino 1983), and internally in the sense that the scientists in the cases she examined shape their conclusions around personal, social, and cultural interests rather than on the basis of the empirical evidence.

Similar patterns can be detected within development practice. For example, Easterly (2013) shows that development aid is often guided by political or pragmatic strategies, while Cooke (2004) argues that Western donors aspire to establish a neoliberal order in the developing world through the management and administration of development efforts (see also Wilson 2006, 503). If there is in fact little difference between how (development) experts and the public reason, it seems that the scientific part of the socioscientific dispute is less esoteric or exclusive than proponents of the positivist view claim.

Proponents of the positivist view could respond that all that the critics have shown is that scientists and experts are fallible, liable to being influenced by political interest and sociocultural values and contexts. They have *not* shown, however, that experts should not strive to adhere to the Mertonian principles. In this way proponents of the positivist position can retain the boundary between scientific and public forms of reasoning and between experts and lay people: good development practice should be free from sociocultural influences, even if this is not always possible in practice.

This then raises the question: is positivist science really the best way of addressing socioscientific issues, such as development? According to its critics, positivism suffers from some serious shortcomings when it comes to socioscientific disputes. Most significant is the objection that the technocratic nature of the positivist view, as Bingle and Gaskell (1994, 191–3) argue, will tend to ignore or even overrule the views of those who are meant to benefit from the scientific input. This trend is similarly present within development. The assumption that the technological and scientific knowledge is superior to local knowledge often leads the technocratic, positivist approach to distort and misrepresent development precisely because it (more or less systematically) excludes local stakeholders—including their sociocultural values and contexts—from the socioscientific process (Beck and Ghosh 2000; Chambers 1995; Craig and Porter 2003; Easterly 2013; Ferguson 1990, 1994). Thus, there is a real need within the development community to move beyond the positivist approach and embrace local knowledge. The second wave of (development) expertise aims to do exactly that.

4.1.2 The Second Wave of Development Expertise: A Social Constructivist View

As a consequence of the critiques raised against the positivist view, some scholars have argued that we should adopt a *social constructivist* view of science and expertise (e.g., Funtowicz and Ravetz 1991; Irwin and Wynne 2003; Jasanoff 1987, 2004; Latour 1987; Longino 1983, 1990; Mulkay 1979; Woolgar 1988; Wynne 1989). Although there are several social constructivist positions (Bingle and Gaskell 1994, 190), they have in common the view that if there can be no politically neutral (socio)scientific solution, as Jasanoff (1987) and Longino (1983) suggest, or if the solution would be impoverished or misrepresentative of the local reality without sociocultural input (Chambers 1995, 1997; Bingle and Gaskell 1994), then we must open up the scientific process and expertise to lay people.

The social constructivist position instantiates the second objection raised against the positivist view, namely that it ignores the fact that lay people may possess important knowledge for socioscientific decision-making. Wynne's (1989) case study of how Cumbrian sheep farmers can contribute to the scientific understanding of the dangers of radioactive fallout is often taken as a paradigmatic example of the need to take a social constructivist view on science and expertise. In his study, Wynne (1989, 37) documents how British government scientists, in the wake of the Chernobyl disaster and its wider impact, systematically failed to acknowledge

> that the farmers held extensive knowledge about sheep habits, the local physical environment, and farming practices and decision-making, all of which needed to be integrated with more abstract and formal scientific knowledge to create an effective response framework to the Chernobyl fallout.

Wynne's example, the proponents of social constructivism argue, shows that we need to democratize science and expertise (Kleinman 2000) because nonscientists may hold embodied or tacit knowledge which can contribute to solving socioscientific issues. If this were true, social constructivists argue, expertise cannot be considered esoteric or privileged. Anyone may thus legitimately contribute to the process.[5]

Within the development literature, the proponents of indigenous knowledge and participatory approaches have advanced similar arguments for the democratization of development expertise (e.g., Agrawal 1995a, 1995b; Chambers 1995, 1997; DeWalt 1994; Sen 2005; Sillitoe 1998, 2004). There are both normative and epistemic reasons for adopting a social constructivist approach to development. Normatively speaking, proponents of social constructivism hold that indigenous, embodied, and tacit forms of knowledge ought to be recognized as legitimate forms of knowledge and expertise on a par with scientific expertise.[6] As Watene and Yap (2015, 53) argue, "[i]f we are serious about the contribution of indigenous peoples, then we must also admit that no serious conversation of indigenous perspectives of sustainable development can take place without it," while Sillitoe (1998, 225) argues that not doing so constitutes a "[l]ack of respect for others' ways," which "leads to offensive interference in their lives."

Epistemically speaking, the argument for adopting a social constructivist approach to development rests on the idea that the involvement of local stakeholders makes for more informed and more responsive development interventions. As Sillitoe (1998, 224) points out, "development initiatives that pay attention to local perceptions and ways are more likely to be relevant to people's needs and to generate sustainable interventions." Bollig and Schulte (1999) and Davis (2005) offer examples of how technological and indigenous knowledge can be incorporated in a holistic response to environmental changes, such as desertification, while Watene and Yap (2015) argue that the holistically focused knowledge of indigenous peoples can contribute to addressing sustainable development.[7]

Critics, however, argue that because social constructivists reject the idea that science can be value-free—that is, science will always, to some extent, be influenced by sociocultural values and contexts as well as the scientists' own strategic interests—the argument seems to relativize not only lay input, such as indigenous knowledge, but also *scientific facts*. If we allow for sociocultural influence, would our scientific facts not be contingent upon such factors as power struggles, economic interests, or personal and cultural beliefs?

One way for social constructivists to respond to this challenge is to admit that scientific knowledge is socially constructed and thus by definition contingent. That does not mean, however, that the social constructivist position cannot evaluate a scientific claim. As Bingle and Gaskell (1994, 191) argue, while there can indeed be no unbiased assessment of the scientific claims in the social constructivist view, citizens are engaged in a process of judging whether the claim in question is influenced by personal, social, economic, or cultural interests to the extent that it is untrustworthy. Thus, in the social constructivist view, scientists have an incentive to present their findings in the most neutral, intelligible, and well-argued manner possible if they want it to be accepted as a scientific fact.

A second critique comes from Collins and Evans (2002, 237; 2008, 9–10), who argue that although social constructivism solves what they call *the problem of legitimacy* it fails adequately to address *the problem of extension*. The problem of legitimacy, according to Collins and Evans, concerns *who* may legitimately claim expertise. Social constructivists solve the problem of legitimacy "by showing that the basis of technical decision-making can and should be widened beyond the core of certified experts" (Collins and Evans 2002, 237). But the problem of extension refers to *how far* participation in technical decision-making should extend beyond the scientific core. Does more participation by definition lead to better (socio)scientific solutions?

The problem of extension arises from the nagging intuition that "there are cases where [. . .] participation by the public should have been *decreased*, because their expertise was insufficient to make a contribution" (Collins and Evans 2002, 263; italics in original). Collins and Evans (2002, 242–6) start from the idea that, at least within what they call the 'esoteric' sciences—sciences which do not have any immediate impact on the public, such as astrophysics—we usually acknowledge that expert authority should only be extended to a core set of specialized scientists. Similarly, in relation to socioscientific issues, for example agricultural practices, there may often be special circumstances which are significant only to trained and experienced specialists.

Proponents of the social constructivist position could object that this only shows the need for more scientific transparency: the public could, and arguably would, be aware of such special circumstances if only they had access to the knowledge of the specialists. However, this lack of knowledge is exactly what Collins and Evans mean to highlight. Although we should not abandon the idea that the public can contribute to (socio)scientific decision-making, the social constructivist position does not provide any meaningful way of distinguishing between appropriate and inappropriate contributions to the (socio)scientific discourse.

To see this, let us consider two possible ways of addressing the issue of extension. First, social constructivists could argue that participation should be limited to those who have a stake in the (socio)scientific issue. This solution may seem sensible in the social constructivist view because it does not make science esoteric—anyone can potentially participate in the technical decision-making process and especially in relation to socioscientific disputes which affect the larger part of the population. However, discriminating along these lines does not secure better (socio) scientific solutions, according to Collins and Evans (2002, 261). Imagine, for example, that a group of London financiers shortly prior to the Chernobyl disaster had bought the land of the Cumbrian sheep farmers in Wynne's case study. For all intents and purposes, the farmers would have transferred their stakeholder rights to participation to the financiers, yet the farmers themselves retain the expertise, which led social constructivists to argue for the extension of expert authority in the first place.

Recognizing this paradox, social constructivists could argue that participation rights should be based on expertise. That is, the farmers ought to be included in the scientific decision-making process because they possess a certain kind of technical knowledge which is relevant to address the particular issue. This solution, however, puts science and expertise squarely back to the positivist approach, to which the social constructivists object. Thus, according to Collins and Evans, we need to move beyond social constructivism without throwing out the baby—the idea that expertise can extend beyond specialized scientists—with the bathwater. What we need, Collins and Evans (2008, 10) argue, is a normative view of expertise, which can answer "how, when, and why, to limit participation in technical decision-making."

In the next sections, I discuss Collins and Evans's (2002, 2008) proposal to address this issue by establishing a normative categorization of expertise and how this categorization may contribute to further our understanding of development expertise and authority.

4.2 Third Wave Expertise

How can we retain the credibility of (socio)scientific decision-making while extending the notion of (development) expertise beyond the core set of specialized and credentialed scientists and experts? Although we recognize that expert authority should belong to specialized experts within certain "esoteric" domains, on socioscientific issues we do want to extend expert authority to members of the public. While Collins and Evans (2002, 261) reject the idea that the public should be granted socioscientific decision-making rights purely by virtue of the impact of the scientific solution on their lives, they propose that such rights should be extended based on expertise. Someone may legitimately contribute to the (socio)scientific process insofar as they possess knowledge about the subject matter. Collins and Evans label this normative view *third wave expertise.*

Collins and Evans (2008, chap. 1) propose categorizing expertise into five levels.[8] An overview of these five levels of knowledge can be found in Table 4.1. According to Collins and Evans, only the contributory and interactional forms of expertise are relevant when extending expert authority.

Humans require language skills, social skills, motor skills, emotional skills, moral skills, and cognitive skills in order to lead a functional life. We may think of these skills as trivial because they are so widely accepted. But it does not change the fact that as human beings we already possess a large body of tacit and embodied knowledge: "things you just know how to do without being able to explain the rules for how you do them" (Collins and Evans 2008, 13). Collins and Evans label this category of knowledge *ubiquitous.*

As Table 4.1 makes clear, the problem with ubiquitous forms of knowledge is that they do not provide a deep enough understanding of the scientific subject matter to allow stakeholders to discriminate between or make judgments about good and bad scientific inputs and decisions. Making such judgments, Collins and Evans (2008, 23–4) argue, requires *specialist tacit knowledge.* The two forms of expertise which Collins and

Table 4.1 Overview of the Five Forms of Knowledge

Ubiquitous forms of expertise			*Specialized forms of expertise*	
Beer-mat knowledge	*Popular understanding of science*	*Primary source knowledge*	*Contributory expertise*	*Interactional expertise*
Knowledge of trivia/fingertip knowledge	*Knowledge acquired from following the news and reading popular books*	*Knowledge that can be gained by primary sources*	*The ability to contribute meaningfully to the scientific discussion of a particular field*	*The ability to interact and communicate meaningfully with the actors of a particular field*
Does not ensure actual understanding of practical application	Does not capture the complexity of scientific debates	Does not provide ability to evaluate information	Does not necessarily provide interactional expertise	Does not necessarily provide contributory expertise

Source: Partly adapted from Collins and Evans (2008, 14)

Evans identify under the heading of specialist tacit knowledge are contributory and interactional expertise.

Contributory expertise is the ability to contribute meaningfully to the scientific discussion of a particular field (Collins and Evans 2002, 254; 2008, 24). Traditionally, we attribute contributory expertise to scientists who are specialized within their field, who know and can distinguish between relevant and irrelevant literature, who know the scientific methods and can judge scientific claims, and who themselves can therefore contribute to the field in a novel way. Additionally, we can also understand contributory expertise as a more tacit or embodied kind of knowledge: "expert status is achieved [when] complete contexts are unselfconsciously recognized and performance is related to them in fluid way using cues that it is impossible to articulate" (Collins and Evans 2008, 24–5). While expertise in this sense is individualist, Collins and Evans (2008, 27) argue that mastering certain skills also requires a certain degree of socialization into the relevant group practices.

From this definition, it is clear how Wynne's sheep farmers can and should be attributed with contributory expertise. Recall that according to Wynne (1989, 37), the sheep farmers held a great deal of experiential knowledge about the ecology of sheep in a mildly radioactive environment, such as their grazing habits and the distribution of radioactive fallout. According to Collins and Evans, this expertise should have qualified the sheep farmers to participation rights in the particular socioscientific decision-making process in response to the radioactive fallout. In this context, Collins and Evans (2008, 255) argue, the sheep farmers exhibited "all the characteristics of core-group experts in terms of experience in the ecology of hill sheep on (mildly radioactive) grassland, even though they had no formal qualifications." However, as Wynne's study shows, the sheep farmers were never properly consulted. Why was this?

Collins and Evans (2002, 254–6) locate the cause of the dispute between the sheep farmers and the government experts to a lack of interactional expertise, which would have allowed the groups to communicate effectively with each other. *Interactional expertise* is defined as the ability to interact and communicate meaningfully with the actors of a particular scientific field (Collins and Evans 2002, 254). For someone to possess interactional expertise, they only need to be able to *speak the language* of the scientific field (Collins and Evans 2008, 28). One can have interactional expertise without having contributory expertise: one does not need to be an expert in the scientific practice in order to be able to communicate with its practitioners. For example, a manager may be able to interact effectively with his employees without necessarily having a deep understanding of their specialist knowledge.

Crucially, as in Wynne's example, one can also have contributory expertise without interactional expertise (Collins and Evans 2002, 255). This was the case for both the sheep farmers as well as their adversaries, the government scientists. Although both groups were evidently experts in some respect on the particular situation and the optimal solution thus required the input of both the government scientists and the sheep farmers (Collins and Evans 2002, 256), cooperation remained elusive due to the lack of capacity by both main groups of actors to communicate and share their knowledge with each other.

Let us call this *the issue of miscommunication*. The issue of miscommunication arises when two or more (groups of) contributory experts lack the interactional expertise to communicate their knowledge to each other because the sources of their expertise are different (e.g., technical versus experiential).[9] In the next section, I argue that the issue of miscommunication is similarly present within a development context, and that adopting Collins and Evan's normative framework of expertise can help us to understand how and why to include local stakeholders in the socio-scientific decision-making process.

4.3 Third Wave Expertise and Development

Can Collins and Evans's idea of third wave expertise and the concepts of interactional and contributory expertise help further our understanding of development expertise? In this section, I argue that Collins and Evans's classification of expertise can help us to (a) determine who should be granted authority as a development expert when setting a development agenda and (b) identify potential sources of miscommunication that arise from this expansion of expert authority. The issue, I hope to show, is a lack of interactional expertise in both, or either, of the external development experts and/or the local stakeholders. Following Collins and Evans, I call this view *third wave development expertise*.

Third wave development expertise starts from the observation that Collins and Evans's diagnosis of the dispute between the sheep farmers and government scientists in Wynne's study is analogous to the relationship within development between external development experts and local stakeholders. The analogy is at least threefold. First, local forms of knowledge have traditionally been underappreciated within development efforts—and hence by development experts and aid donors—compared to the more technical knowledge of the traditionally accepted development experts. As I have indicated, this has led some development scholars to argue for a broader and earlier inclusion of local stakeholders in the decision-making process. Second, such expansion of development expertise gives rise to the problem of extension: how far should expert authority be extended beyond the traditional core of development experts? The concept of contributory expertise can help us determine this question. Third, as in Wynne's study, both lay experts (local stakeholders with relevant tacit, embodied, or indigenous knowledge) and external, technical experts may suffer from a lack of interactional expertise, causing miscommunication between the two parties. As the first of these observations—that expert authority should be extended beyond the traditional core of development experts—has already been analyzed in section 1.2, I focus in the following on the last two observations.

The third wave of development expertise follows Collins and Evans in recognizing the social constructivists' claim that we need to extend expertise beyond the core set of technical experts. That is, development expertise should not only be attributed to the traditional group of development experts but also to local stakeholders. As I have argued there are both normative and epistemic reasons for this expansion of development expertise. Normatively speaking, it would be democratically illegitimate to exclude local stakeholders from the decision-making process because the resulting development agenda will have an impact on their lives, while, epistemically speaking, local stakeholders may hold tacit, embodied, and indigenous knowledge which is important to ensure socioculturally and contextually sensitive development initiatives.

However, the expansion of authority in terms of development expertise raises the issue that not all local stakeholders have something valuable to contribute to the development agenda, at least at a (socio)scientific level. While the Cumbrian sheep farmers did indeed have something significant to contribute to the socioscientific issue of radioactive downfall, this would arguably not be the case for a group of London investors or local construction workers in the same scenario. Why is this so? As Collins and Evans argue, whereas the sheep farmers had knowledge relating to the impact of radioactive downfall on sheep farming, this could hardly be said of the other groups.

It is also the case when extending expert authority in regard to development that some stakeholders hold relevant knowledge while others do not. Although city dwellers should definitely be granted expert authority when it comes to addressing urban reforms, I contend that involving them in questions of agricultural development would be counterproductive. Most city dwellers have little to no knowledge about agricultural practices. If this is so, there are good reasons for applying Collins and Evans's normative view of expertise to development expertise, which only extends expert authority to stakeholders with contributory expertise—those who have relevant experience on the different aspects of development.

It would be naïve, however, to think that everyone would be able to contribute meaningfully in regard to all aspects of development, such as education, agriculture, healthcare, sanitation, urban planning, economic growth, labor opportunities, social welfare, human rights, to name a few. Indeed, the term 'development expert' covers a wide range of more specialized experts—such as development economists, development ethicists, healthcare specialists, agricultural specialists, water management experts, human rights lawyers and scholars, humanitarian aid practitioners, and so on—who can only claim contributory expertise within their specialized field (although we should recognize that some may be specialized in multiple relevant fields, of course). A consequence of this is that different aspects of development require the involvement of different contributory experts, broadly conceived to include both technical specialist experts as well as holders of local knowledge.

Decision-making within development thus involves a variety of participants, which creates the risk of miscommunication. Not only does the process involve different specializations but each group of specialized experts are also divided into technical experts, on the one hand, and experiential experts, on the other. Along each divide—specialization and kind of knowledge—the different groups of experts may communicate through their own specialist language each with their own tacit and underlying assumptions, methods, and aims. In other words, although the different experts may have interactional expertise within their own domain and relative to their kind of knowledge (technical or experiential), their interactional expertise does not necessarily translate into the ability to participate in, contribute to, or interact within and in regard to the discussions on the other aspects of development.[10]

Without cross-cutting interactional expertise, there is a real risk that the various expert parties may talk past each other or ignore one another's input. In such cases, the discussion tends to revert to the default setting, namely a preference for technical language and methodology (and, consequentially, technocratic solutions). Even if both parties have knowledge which can contribute to the (socio)scientific field, the parties may fail to merge their knowledge due to a lack of communication skills.

How can this situation be mitigated? Fortunately, the concept of interactional expertise may offer a solution. Recall that for someone to have interactional expertise, it was only required that they were able to speak the language of the specialists and *not* that they actually had contributory expertise. Thus, in situations where one or more of the parties in a (socio) scientific dispute lack interactional expertise, they should be represented by someone who *does* possess enough interactional expertise to mediate between the parties (Collins and Evans 2002, 256). Let us label this role of the interactionally proficient expert *the mediating expert* (my term, not Collins and Evans's). In the following section, I turn to identifying five types of mediating experts who can help advance the socioscientific discussion on development.

4.4 Five Types of Mediating Expertise

I concluded the previous section by arguing, following Collins and Evans, that a lack of interactional expertise may lead to a dispute between two (or more) contributory expert parties on a given (socio)scientific issue, such as a development agenda. I further claimed that employing what

I call "mediating experts" could ameliorate this issue. The role of the mediating expert is to make the knowledge and arguments of the different parties in the (socio)scientific dispute intelligible in the language of their adversaries. In order to fulfill this role, the mediating expert must possess at least two kinds of ability in order to perform her role successfully, namely translation and discrimination (Collins and Evans 2002, 257–9). *Translation* is the ability to communicate between different frames of reference: to make a statement expressed within one social and linguistic world intelligible to the members of another social and linguistic framework. The mediating expert must have interactional expertise within both frames of reference.

Discrimination is the ability to distinguish between genuine experts—those with contributory expertise—and nonexperts. Collins and Evans (2008, 68–9) propose that the discrimination of expertise should be based on *experience*: does the person making the claim to expertise have any experience within the field she claims to be an expert in? As the definition of contributory expertise makes clear, there can be no expertise without experience. Experience in this sense is what distinguishes Wynne's sheep farmers from the general public in regard to expertise in sheep farming on mildly radioactive land, and it is why development expertise should be extended to local stakeholders.

Brand and Karvonen (2007, 26–9) distinguish between four types of mediating expertise within (sustainable) development. Each of these four types of mediating experts contributes to development (and in our context, the setting of a development agenda) by bringing different stakeholders together, making their claims intelligible to the various stakeholders, and searching out common ground between them. The four types of mediating experts which Brand and Karvonen identify are the outreach expert, the interdisciplinary expert, the meta-expert, and the civic expert. I propose that we should add a fifth type of mediating expert, whom I label the *political expert*. Let me briefly explain each type of mediating expert in turn.

The aim of the *outreach expert*, according to Brand and Karvonen (2007, 26), is to communicate and disseminate scientific knowledge to the public and thereby increase their level of knowledge and information. Such knowledge may in turn help the public make informed decisions, both politically as well as in interaction with external experts. One way of challenging the scientific conservatism of development experts is to foster collaboration between different specialist experts. This is the role of the *interdisciplinary expert* who works across disciplines and investigates where insights from one pool of knowledge can contribute to creating solutions within another discipline (Brand and Karvonen 2007, 26–7). Given that we have broadened the scope of what we mean by scientific knowledge to include culturally embedded forms of knowledge, one task of the interdisciplinary expert is to communicate not only between traditional scientific disciplines but also between different cultural frames of reference.

Not all scientific fields or their experts can or should contribute to development, however. The role of the *meta-expert* is to make judgments as to who can potentially contribute to the socioscientific discussion and solution (Brand and Karvonen 2007, 27–8). The two abilities outlined above—translation and discrimination—are especially important in order for the meta-expert to function properly: on the one hand, the meta-expert must be able to discriminate between relevant and irrelevant contributions to the discussion; on the other hand, she must be able to translate the insights of one field of expertise into another in order to "identify potential linkages and facilitate their co-discovery" (Brand and Karvonen 2007, 28).

These three types of mediating experts fail to address the issue which is central to this chapter, however, namely that not all experts belong to the core-set of specialized scientists: they do nothing to challenge the traditional top-down view of development expertise and the privileged position of the so-called development expert and thus uphold and exacerbate the asymmetric relationship of power between external experts and scientists on the one hand, and local stakeholders on the other.

Two additional mediating experts may be essential in order to mitigate this asymmetry. First, Brand and Karvonen (2007, 28–9) propose to ameliorate this issue by adding a fourth type of mediating development expert, the *civic expert*. The role of the civic expert is to engage with the public in order to inform the socioscientific decision-making process with their experiential knowledge—what has been admitted as tacit or embodied contributory development expertise in the third wave. In this way, the civic expert fosters and encourages public participation in the socioscientific decision-making and deliberation with "credentialed" experts (Brand and Karvonen 2007, 28). In this way, the civic expert recognizes the twofold nature of development and the setting of a development agenda, which requires both technical and sociocultural input (DeWalt 1994), and works to break down the asymmetric power relation between technical experts and lay experts.

Second, while Brand and Karvonen's four types of mediating expertise certainly help us to envision how the third wave of development expertise can be realized in practice, I believe it misses a crucial aspect of development, namely the political. Brand and Karvonen's four types of expert only operate within the advisory domain and are focused on bringing technical experts and lay experts together to form a socioscientific solution. There may be individuals and groups who have been left out of the socioscientific decision-making process because they were found unfit to claim expert authority, such as the local construction workers who arguably possess little knowledge of sheep farming on mildly radioactive land. Yet, the socioscientific solution (e.g., the development agenda) will often also impact on or implicate stakeholders who have not been part of the socioscientific decision-making process, such as aid donors, politicians, and locals with no particular (formal or tacit) expertise. In other words, the group of people who can claim scientific decision-making rights is smaller than the group of people who can claim political decision-making rights.

This discrepancy in membership creates the scenario in which a both socioculturally and technically sensitive solution, developed within the (socio)scientific domain, is overruled within the political domain. This is, of course, in the very nature of the political process. But, we may ask, can we not do more to ensure a better fate for our (hopefully carefully crafted) solution? One way of doing so is by appointing someone to mediate between experts (including lay experts) and the broader spectrum of political participants. I call this type of mediating expert the *political expert*. The political expert is both scientifically and politically adept—in other words, has interactional expertise within both domains—and can show how and in what ways the socioscientific solution is politically significant and what is at stake in adopting it as a matter of public policy. Therefore, the political expert creates a link between the scientific and political domains while acknowledging the privileged status of the political process over the scientific.

Employing these five mediating experts could have made a difference in the dispute between Wynne's sheep farmers and the government scientists. The outreach expert would have been able to communicate the concerns of the government scientists to the sheep farmers, pre-empting the distrust which arose because the government scientists were perceived to have ignored the local reality of sheep farming. The interdisciplinary expert could have fostered further collaboration between the two stakeholder groups and shown where the insights of the farmers could have contributed to the scientific understanding of the situation. The meta-expert would have been able to make the government scientists aware from the outset that the sheep farmers possessed relevant knowledge. The civic expert could have helped make explicit the experiential knowledge of the sheep farmers, enriching the socioscientific pool of knowledge to include insights into the local pragmatic practices of sheep farming on mildly radioactive soil. Finally, the political expert could have calmed some of the worries of the greater public about the safety of consuming Cumbrian sheep meat, for example by urging politicians not to draw rash conclusions based on what was a deeply flawed socioscientific process.

4.5 Three Objections to Third Wave (Development) Expertise

Third wave (development) expertise aims to delimit who can legitimately claim authority as an expert. Expert authority, this view holds, should be extended based on whether local stakeholders possess relevant (tacit, embodied, or indigenous) knowledge that can contribute meaningfully to the socioscientific issue of setting a development agenda. However, restricting expert authority in this way leads to three objections that social constructivists can raise: first, it ignores insights from nonexperts; second, it ignores the epistemic role of the unregulated public sphere; and, third, it leads to epistemic injustice. In the following section, I explain and address each of these objections in turn.

4.5.1 The Objection from Spontaneous Knowledge Creation

The first objection that social constructivists can raise against third wave (development) expertise is that it closes off the possibility of unexpected yet valuable insights from members of the public who cannot claim expert authority on the third wave view. We cannot always know, this objection holds, where scientific insights come from and, hence, we cannot justify excluding members of the public at large from having authority within the socioscientific decision-making process. Only by adopting the social constructivist view, which does not discriminate between experts and the public, can we ensure that such unexpected insights are considered in the decision-making process. A good example of this is Boyan Slat, who has pioneered an innovative technology for cleaning up plastic waste from the oceans.[11] A mere high school student at the time of innovation, Slat would arguably not have been granted expert authority on the third wave view of (development) expertise.

How can the third wave view of (development) expertise accommodate such unexpected contributions? There are at least three mechanisms by which third wave (development) expertise can and does incorporate insights from members of the general public, such as Boyan Slat. First of all, it is important to note that there is a distinction between contributing to a field and being a contributory expert within that field (Collins and Evans 2008, 70). Even though Slat was not a contributory expert within the particular field of ocean cleanup, he could still make a contribution insofar as he possessed interactional expertise within that field so he could relay his insights to the experts or, conversely, someone within the field could have picked up his insights. Making a contribution to the field would not automatically make Slat a contributory expert (Collins and Evans 2008, 73).

However, second, both expertise and scientific domains are dynamic concepts on the third wave view. In the first case, just because Slat was not an expert on ocean cleanup *before* he embarked on his innovative project, there is no reason why he should not be granted expert authority insofar as his contribution is recognized as valuable and founded on an actual understanding of the subject matter. In the second case, as Collins and Evans (2008, 73) argue, such recognition “can lead to the novel contributory expertise coming to be a regular part of the esoteric domain." As such, it is the boundaries of the domain (e.g., ocean cleanup technology) that are expanded (in turn expanding what it means to have expertise within this domain).

Thus, third, we must insist that any member of the public can potentially contribute to and transform the socioscientific domain. The idea behind third wave (development) expertise is not to deliberately ignore input from the public but to discriminate between inputs that can and do make a contribution and those that cannot and do not. Consider, for example, the hypothetical case in which Slat was a hoaxer whose innovative ocean cleanup mechanism was based on pseudoscience, which meant that the mechanism was useless in practice.[12] Likewise, we could imagine that Slat had less sinister motives but was merely so incompetent in predicting ocean currents or calculating the costs of implementation that the mechanism would be useless or unfeasible. Arguably, in such cases we would hesitate to grant that Slat was an expert or that he was making an actual contribution to the field. What these hypothetical cases show is that even if we recognize that contributions can come from unexpected sources, we still need to make judgments about such contributions and distinguish good from bad contributions. The social constructivist view, as argued, does not provide any meaningful way of making such distinctions.

4.5.2 The Objection from the Unregulated Public Sphere

The second objection that social constructivists can raise holds that proponents of third wave (development) expertise forget or ignore the importance of what Habermas (1989, 1996) and Taylor (1993) refer to as the *public sphere*. The public sphere, according to Habermas and Taylor, is the fluid space—for example print media (newspapers, books, and magazines), town-hall meetings, television news and discussion shows, discussion forums on the internet, op-eds and commentary sections, public demonstrations, and public lectures—where individuals come together to raise, question, reflect on, debate, reason about, and agree on matters of public concern and interest. In other words, the public sphere is where public reasoning and the formation of public opinion on common concerns regarding public policy take place.

It is clear that the public sphere is compatible with and an important part of the democratic and inclusive republican account of political authority that I developed in the previous chapter. Sen (1999a, 8; 1999b, 152), for example, has often argued that some of the worst famines of the twentieth century could have been mitigated if the relevant governing bodies had to confront a free public sphere with independent media and freedom of expression, while Bicchieri and Marini (2015) show how open debates about social norms, such as female genital mutilation, are crucial in eliminating damaging social practices.

How the public sphere relates to the (socio)scientific domain, in which I have argued we should prefer a third wave approach, is less clear, however. It seems that there is an overlap between the role of the public sphere and the (socio)scientific domain insofar as the public sphere serves an epistemic role by providing a forum where the public can raise and respond to knowledge claims.

The crucial point of the objection from the unregulated public sphere is the notion that the public sphere can best be categorized as unruly: it is open, inclusive to all, and unregulated in terms of the topics that are discussed (Habermas 1989, 1, 36–7). If this is so, the objection goes, there seems to be a tension between the public sphere on the one hand, and the concept of third wave (development) expertise on the other hand, which limits who can legitimately contribute to the socioscientific discussion to those who have contributory experience. In other words, insofar as the public sphere serves an epistemic purpose and insofar as it cannot (or should not) be regulated, it seems that the attempt to regulate the process of (socio)scientific decision-making by adopting the normative account of third wave (development) expertise is mistaken. Only the social constructivist position, this objection continues, can adequately accommodate the unruliness of the public sphere because it fully embraces the public construction of knowledge.

Thus, we need to ask, first, how does the public sphere relate to the (socio)scientific domain and, second, to what extent is this relationship a challenge to the third wave view of (development) expertise? In the following, I first give an account of how the public sphere relates to the domain of (socio)scientific decision-making before I argue that while the public sphere is indeed intricately connected to the (socio)scientific domain, there are good reasons to keep the two domains distinct.

What is the relationship between the public sphere and (socio)scientific decision-making? Edwards (1999, 164) provides an account of the public sphere in relation to scientific practice. In particular, he identifies three 'institutional categories'[13]—the media, social movements, and participatory forums—within which the public acts "as an intermediary structure between scientific expertise and policy making." The three institutions each play a dual role in relation to the (socio)scientific domain: on the one hand, through them the public can raise concerns that they want to put on the scientific agenda; on the other hand, they can communicate or incorporate scientific findings that then serve as input to the democratic process of public policy-making.

An independent and free press certainly serves as an important tool for development by acting as a voice of the poor and vulnerable and holding the governing bodies accountable—as, for example, in Sen's study of famines. In relation to the (socio)scientific domain, the media may likewise help to put items of public concern on the scientific agenda and, conversely, communicate scientific knowledge as input to the public deliberation. In other words, in a development perspective, the media can help create a critical link between development experts, the public, and political decision-makers.[14]

Social movements, according to Edwards (1999, 167), aim to "mobilise the public, to articulate problems and issues and to influence the public and political agenda." In this way, social movements are a powerful means in the political empowerment of local stakeholders.[15] Although social movements primarily aim to influence public policy (and thus primarily operate within the political domain), they also relate to the (socio)scientific domain by lobbying to put social issues on the scientific agenda. A good example of this is the AIDS activists in San Francisco in the 1980s, who were successful in putting research on AIDS treatment on the scientific agenda (Epstein 1995, 1996; Collins and Evans 2002, 262).

Lastly, *participatory forums*, as I hope to have shown in this chapter, are essential within socioscientific decision-making. Such forums allow the experts to incorporate local insights and knowledge, and the locals to learn from and evaluate the insights of the experts. Consequently, in recent years, participatory development—the active inclusion of local stakeholders in development processes—has become an invaluable tool to foster mutual learning and accountability between local stakeholders and development experts.

How do the public and the public sphere contribute to the specific task of setting a development agenda? Edwards' taxonomy shows that the public sphere mainly serves to link the political and the socioscientific domains, which I have argued are both central to development policymaking. In regard to a development agenda, this intermediary role plays out in two important respects. First, the public sphere is crucial (although not solely responsible) for the *identification* of social issues that are relevant for a development agenda. When the public sphere overlaps with the local stakeholders, it provides a valuable insight into local circumstances, needs, and ways of life, which may be incorporated at either the political or the (socio)scientific level or both of them. Second, the public is largely responsible for *lobbying*—through both formal (e.g., petitions, the media) and informal (e.g., protests, public art) means—to put these issues on the political and (socio)scientific agendas. This is what is implied by the claim to local authority: that local stakeholders—the public—have a say in what social, environmental, (socio)scientific, and political issues a development agenda should address.

It is obvious that the public sphere plays an important role in knowledge creation and (socio)scientific decision-making, both in general as well as in a development perspective. However, the openness and unruliness of the public sphere seems to be in tension with the regulated and normative view of expertise that the third wave embodies. That is, as social constructivists would argue, if knowledge creation and (socio)scientific decision-making benefit epistemically from being discussed within an unregulated public sphere, it would be mistaken to try and limit who can contribute to the (socio)scientific domain in the way that proponents of the third wave view of (development) expertise advocate.

How should we respond to this charge? First of all, we need to acknowledge that the tension can likely not be avoided: while opening up the (socio)scientific decision-making to the wider public may at times bring about better decisions, there will also be other times when the public will make worse decisions than the trained experts. In fact, third wave (development) expertise seems to embrace this tension. On the one hand, third wave (development) expertise acknowledges that (socio)scientific decision-making can and does benefit from an extension of the range of contributors to include local stakeholders. On the other hand, however, it would be naïve to dismiss the notion of expertise. Experts do have an intricate and in-depth knowledge about particular subjects; sometimes members of the broader public can claim such knowledge, but at other times they cannot. As I hope to have argued in this chapter, at least in matters of their own development there will often be a great overlap between the public sphere and the domain of expertise.

However, as Edwards (1999, 168) argues, we need to distinguish between *influencing* the (socio)scientific agenda and *contributing* to its decision-making process. While the former concerns *what* should be on the (socio)scientific research agenda, the latter concerns *how* this research should proceed. Within the third wave view, the role of the public sphere is primarily reserved for the task of influencing the research agenda because, as argued, a greater public involvement does not always improve the (socio)scientific decision-making.

Hence, at least analytically and normatively, and often empirically, we need to distinguish between the public sphere and the domain of experts. Accounting for the public sphere is not so much an argument for dissolving the domain of expertise as much as it, as Edwards (1999, 169; emphasis added) concludes, "underlines *the importance of a careful management of boundaries* between the spheres of scientific expertise, public discussion and decision-making on policies." This is exactly what the notion of third wave (development) expertise sets out to do.

4.5.3 The Objection from Epistemic Injustice

The third objection that social constructivists can raise holds that third wave (development) expertise leads to two particular forms of epistemic injustice, namely *testimonial injustice* and *hermeneutical injustice*.[16] In short, testimonial injustice is the idea that we may attribute more or less credibility to a statement based on prejudices about the speaker, such as gender, social background, ethnicity, race, sexuality, tone of voice, accent, and so on (Fricker 2007, 1, sec. 1.3). An example of this may be when "the police do not believe you because you are black" (Fricker

2007, 1). Hermeneutical injustice occurs whenever these prejudices structurally affect what can be known and, hence, how someone can make sense of her social experiences (Fricker 2007, 1, sec. 7.1). Someone may, for example, suffer sexual harassment or depression yet be unaware of this because the collective pool of knowledge lacks the concepts of sexual harassment and depression (Fricker 2007, 1, 149).

Testimonial injustices can lead to hermeneutical injustices (Fricker 2007, 162). Consider, for example, how indigenous peoples are often excluded from influencing development. On a structural scale, the exclusion of indigenous peoples (a testimonial injustice) leads to the omission of their perspective in the collective pool of knowledge that is used to shape development efforts. This has the effect that indigenous peoples are rendered unable to communicate their perspectives intelligibly within the existing development discourses (a hermeneutical injustice) because the concepts they may use to describe their experiences are lacking from these discourses qua the previous structural exclusion. Because third wave (development) expertise will exclude some people from the socioscientific decision-making process, this objection goes, it invariably leads to both forms of epistemic injustice.

While we should acknowledge that third wave (development) expertise is vulnerable to both forms of epistemic injustice, I contend that we need to distinguish between epistemic *inequality* and epistemic *injustice*. That is, although the third wave view of (development) expertise might lead to the epistemic inequalities, there are good reasons why they do not constitute epistemic injustices.

First of all, proponents of third wave (development) expertise must bite the bullet on this objection: it is clear how the third wave view of (development) expertise is vulnerable to both kinds of epistemic injustice. In the case of testimonial injustice, the view does distribute credibility unequally when distinguishing contributory experts from nonexperts. In the case of hermeneutical injustice, by restricting the extent to which nonexperts can take part in the socioscientific decision-making process, third wave (development) expertise does run the risk of unequally excluding certain stakeholders from the collective creation of knowledge and, hence, the extent to which they can communicate their experiences intelligibly.

Whether these inequalities constitute *injustices* is less clear, however. In fact, it seems that both kinds of epistemic inequality would only be unjust insofar as we adopt the social constructivist view. That is, the second objection only holds if we accept that, on the one hand, it is illegitimate to attribute different levels of credibility to different speakers and, on the other hand, that all input to the socioscientific decision-making process is valuable or relevant.

However, both of these claims have been disputed in this chapter *at least in relation to the socioscientific decision-making process*. First, it has been argued that we have good reasons to attribute more credibility to certain stakeholders—that is, those with contributory expertise—namely in order to ensure better socioscientific decisions. In other words, not all input is valuable or relevant because it does not add to or may be detrimental to the quality of the solution. Thus, the inequality in terms of testimonial credibility is not based on prejudices about the speaker[17] but rather on a qualified judgment about the value or relevance of the input in relation to the particular task; in this case the setting of a development agenda. Hence, at least in this case, the testimonial inequality does not constitute a testimonial injustice.

Second, even *if* the third wave view of (development) expertise leads to testimonial inequality, it does not necessarily follow that a hermeneutical injustice is done. I have shown how the employment of a set of mediating experts can ameliorate situations in which the perspective of some stakeholders is absent from the development discourse and, by extension, that they cannot make themselves intelligible within this discourse. In fact, the role of the mediating expert is to bring out—*make intelligible*—and translate the tacit or embodied knowledge of the particular stakeholder(s). As such, hermeneutical inequalities and injustices are actually addressed and actively combatted within third wave (development) expertise.

Third and finally, it is crucial to recognize that even though third wave (development) expertise delimits who can legitimately contribute to the socioscientific decision-making process and what constitutes a legitimate contribution, these restrictions do not apply at the *political* level where, as I have argued in Chapter 3, all—especially local—stakeholders should be granted a degree of authority. Thus, the vulnerability to the two forms of epistemic injustice is only present within one particular domain related to the setting of a development agenda.

4.6 Concluding Remarks

This chapters and Chapter 3 have sought to answer the second question that I set out in this book: Who should be involved in the setting of a development agenda? Who has the authority to decide on what goals we should pursue as a matter of development? In Chapter 3, I argued that we can distinguish a claim within the development literature to grant local stakeholders more authority. I further argued that this claim should be interpreted in two ways: as a claim to political authority and as a claim to expert authority. In Chapter 3, I further addressed the claim to local political authority by grounding it in republican theory, while this chapter has dealt with the claim as a claim to expert authority.

In this chapter, I have presented a view of development expertise that I call *third wave development expertise*. Third wave development expertise extends expert authority on development issues—in the present context, the issue of setting a development agenda—beyond the traditional set of development experts to include local stakeholders who possess *contributory expertise*. Someone has contributory expertise insofar as she possesses relevant tacit, embodied, or indigenous knowledge that can contribute meaningfully to the socioscientific issue of setting a development agenda.

The extension of expert authority presents us with the issue of miscommunication between the different stakeholders—that is, between the external development experts and the local lay experts, as well as between the broader set of political decision-makers. The issue of miscommunication, I argued, arises because the different stakeholders lack what Collins and Evans refer to as *interactional expertise*: the ability to translate their knowledge claims into the language of their counterparts and thereby communicate effectively with each other. In response to the issue of miscommunication, I followed Collins and Evans in arguing that employing mediating experts who possess interactional expertise and can bring the different stakeholders together can ameliorate such cases of miscommunication. Five types of mediating experts were identified and explicated upon: the outreach expert, the interdisciplinary expert, the meta-expert, and the civic expert were adopted from Brand and Karvonen, while I added a fifth type, namely the political expert.

Notes

1 The term should not be confused with third wave *economic* development, which refers to the broadening of the foundation for economic development (Bradshaw and Blakely 1999).

2 It is important to note that my adoption of Collins and Evans's notion of third wave expertise is based on my argument that it can help us explain and solve a prominent issue within development, and *not* on the assumption that the notion is the best overall description or analytical conception of expertise compared to the positivist and social constructivist views. Unfortunately, due to constraints of space, I am not able to engage in a more extensive discussion of the justification and applicability of these views in general.

3 In his influential essay, "The Normative Structure of Science," Merton (1973) identifies and explicates four principles or norms of "good science": universality, communalism, disinterestedness, and organized skepticism. These have later come to be known as the Mertonian principles, which help guide legitimate scientific practice (Macfarlane and Cheng 2008).

4 I define 'esoteric' here as something that is in practice only accessible to a select number of people.

5 The public may participate in the scientific process to various degrees and at different stages (Lengwiler 2008, 187–8).

6 This does not entail that the local knowledge claims should be uncritically accepted (or, conversely, rejected), just as scientific knowledge claims should not be accepted by virtue of being 'scientific.' Rather, it implies that we need to recognize that local knowledge claims may have some socioscientific truth and they cannot be dismissed merely because they are not derived from scientific inquiry. Hence, local norms and practices are still subject to scrutiny and criticism.

7 DeWalt (1994) stresses that technological and indigenous knowledge should be seen as complementary inputs to the same solution, rather than as antagonistic and incompatible – a view which is also acknowledged by most contemporary proponents of indigenous knowledge and participation.

8 Collin and Evans's categorization is based especially on Collins's extensive research within the sociology of scientific knowledge (SSK).

9 In practice, the issue of miscommunication may translate into differences in terms of the epistemological and ontological assumptions the different parties employ, in terms of power, as well as in practical disagreements (Brand and Karvonen 2007, 22–4).

10 For a discussion on some of the practical challenges of interacting across different levels, see Cash et al. (2006).

11 For a short biography of Slat, see www.boyanslat.com.

12 See Collins and Evans (2008, 54–7) for a discussion of the case of hoaxers and frauds.

13 This label does not necessarily imply, however, that they are *formal* institutions. Rather, the three institutional categories cover the wide range of informal, unstructured, and dynamic forms of public communicative practices that tend to become *generalized* into certain channels of communication or communicative institutions, such as the media, social movements, and participatory forums. Consider, for example, how the category of the media would include more formal media institutions, such as specific news corporations, as well as informal and often unregulated media outlets, such as op-eds, online blogs, and debate forums.

14 Despite the advantages, the biggest problem with the media, as Edwards (1999, 167) argues and that I, following the work of Collins and Evans, have alluded to earlier in this chapter, is that it is *bias producing*. This is so in two ways. First, the media is motivated not (only) by the common interest or a commitment to the common good but also by commercial interests. What gets taken up in the media—either as a matter of scientific input to the public sphere or in terms of putting certain concerns on the scientific agenda—is often dependent on what 'sells,' creating a bias for sensational findings or overblown fears. Second, as Collins and Evans also argue, the media has a tendency to simplify or even distort scientific findings because of commercial interests. For this reason, the media does not always act as a reliable source of scientific information.

15 For similar conclusions, see, for example, Deneulin and Dinerstein (2010) and Woodward et al. (2011).

16 In general, *epistemic injustice* is the idea that there can be unfair distributions of certain goods that are epistemic in nature, such as (access to) education and information (Fricker 2007, 1). The unequal access to such sources of knowledge means that some people are unfairly disadvantaged in terms of being able to claim expertise. As Fricker (2007, 1) further argues, however, from this definition of epistemic injustice "it seems largely incidental that the good in question can be characterized as an epistemic good" compared, that is, to other goods, such as democratic rights or economic opportunities. Instead, Fricker distinguishes between two distinctively epistemic injustices, namely testimonial and hermeneutical, which cannot be reduced to unfair distribution of goods in general.

17 Unless, of course, we hold the view that it is prejudiced to distinguish between good and bad, better and worse, and substantiated and unsubstantiated arguments—a view that, it seems, would make any deliberative exercise a nonstarter.

5 Four Criteria for the Selection of Human Development Goals

Human development is primarily concerned with what people are able to do or be (i.e., their capabilities and functionings) rather than with the resources and public goods (including merely formal rights and freedoms) that they possess. Crucially, what people are able to do or be and which doings and beings that are normatively relevant may differ from person to person and between different socioeconomic and environmental contexts. Which capabilities and functionings that are normatively relevant is not a given, however, and as I argued in Chapters 3 and 4, it is a question that depends on the input from local stakeholders in addition to aid donors, development experts, policy-makers, and NGOs.

Accordingly, one of the main tasks of applying the capability approach within development is the selection of normatively relevant capabilities and functionings. Unfortunately, both the development and capability literature offer little guidance in this respect. This chapter will fill this lacuna and contribute to both sets of literature by identifying four general criteria that a selection of capabilities and functionings for development should satisfy:

- *Criterion of methodological justification*: A suitable method should be justifiable within the norms of its methodological discipline(s).
- *Criterion of normative justification*: A suitable method should be able to justify its methodology and its list of capabilities and functionings according to normative theory.
- *Criterion of democratic legitimacy*: A suitable method should be sensitive to the will of the people to whom it applies and not impose its list on them.
- *Criterion of contextual sensitivity*: A suitable method should be sensitive to local and nonideal sociocultural, economic, and environmental circumstances and conditions.

The chapter is structured as follows: In the first section (5.1) I introduce the issue of selecting capabilities. In the second section (5.2) I discuss Robeyns's (2003, 70–1) influential set of five criteria that need to be respected when selecting capabilities and argue that these criteria require modification and further specification when applied to the context of development. Consequently, in the subsequent sections (5.3–5.6) I propose, discuss, and specify four general criteria that we should adhere to when selecting capabilities and functionings relevant in a development context.

5.1 Selecting Capabilities

The capability approach is the normative view that human well-being is best conceived of in terms of capabilities and functionings. Capabilities are the real freedom people have to achieve certain doings and beings; functionings are capabilities that have been realized. Real freedom in this sense means that people have the positive preconditions as well as the formal freedom and rights to achieve these doings and beings (i.e., turn them into functionings) if they so wish. A central issue in the application of the capability approach, both in general and applied to development purposes, is the selection of normatively relevant capabilities.

Why do we need to select capabilities? There are at least two positive arguments for this: one normative, the other practical. First of all, we need to make a selection of relevant capabilities for normative reasons. The capability approach is concerned both with well-being freedom and agency freedom.[1] Well-being freedom is the capability people have to achieve goals that, presumably, contribute to their well-being, while agency freedom is conceived as the freedom to pursue any goal regardless of whether it contributes to one's well-being (Sen 1985, 203–4). In short, the difference can be exemplified as someone who can choose between a well-paid job that puts food on the table or to pursue the advancement of global justice at the expense of her own well-being.

The example shows two things. First, the freedom to pursue one's agential goals is obviously valuable regardless of whether it brings about greater well-being. However, second, the example also shows that the capability approach cannot be reduced to merely be concerned with people's freedom to pursue their agential goals. As Sen (1985, 206; italics in original) stresses, both well-being freedom and agency freedom are *essential* for the capability approach:[2]

> [T]he important thing to recognize is that the well-being aspect and the agency aspect of persons have dissimilar roles in moral accounting [. . .] At the risk of oversimplification it can be said that the well-being aspect of a person is important in assessing a person's *advantage*, whereas the agency aspect is important in assessing what a person can do in line with his or her conception of *the good*. The ability to do more good need not be to the person's advantage.

Because of this dual concern, not only with agential goals, but also with people's well-being, capability theorists have normative reasons to claim that we need a selection of relevant capabilities. Consider, for example, how some agential capabilities are detrimental to the well-being of either or both oneself and others, such as smoking in public places or the capability to pollute. Most capability theorists hold that it would be absurd to insist that we do not need to restrict or seek to minimize such potentially harmful capabilities (e.g., Holland 2008). Normatively, then, capability theorists have a reason to engage in the selection of valuable/relevant capabilities and functionings because they are not merely concerned with people's agential freedom but also with their well-being.

Practically speaking, too, capability theorists have a reason to make a selection of capabilities and functionings. The notion of capabilities and functionings is conceptually neutral and thus comprises morally good, morally bad, and morally neutral doings and beings alike (Robeyns 2011). However, the capability approach, as Robeyns (2011, 2016, 2017) further argues, is merely a theoretical *framework*, which can be applied to more specific domains (e.g., empirical studies) or developed into more specific normative theories. The capability approach does not *itself* specify how to apply the framework or which capabilities and functionings may be said to be normatively relevant in this regard.

Thus, capability theorists must themselves fill in the blanks when applying the capability framework, and one of the first questions they should ask is what doings and beings are relevant for their specific application. Even if it is the answer that all (possible) capabilities and functionings are normatively relevant, this constitutes a selection. Often, however, the particular application will only be concerned with a subset of capabilities and functionings depending on, as Robeyns (2011, 2016, 2017) argues, the socioeconomic context, the area of interest, or the normative theory endorsed. An empirical investigation of a community's access to water will most likely not be interested in people's capability to play video games while it is questionable whether a capability theory of democracy would demand that people have the capability to run a marathon in order to be democratically capable.

Although the specification of relevant capabilities is an important task, it is not straightforward to determine which capabilities matter. The capability approach holds that human beings are diverse. Not only do they live in different societies with different social norms and environmental circumstances, they have personal goals in life that they wish to pursue. The capability approach reflects this diversity by acknowledging that there is a plurality of valuable and relevant capabilities and that their value is relative to the personal and socioeconomic circumstances (Robeyns 2005a; 2011). In short, the capability approach recognizes that the substance and content of capability lists may differ between societies as well as between different applications of the capability framework.

This has led capability theorists to argue that we need a selection of relevant capabilities and functionings when applying the capability approach in practice.

For all of these reasons—because different domains and different contexts demand different specific capabilities and functionings—the various applications of the capability approach have traditionally been accompanied by a selection of relevant capabilities and functionings when applied in practice.

Several methods for the selection of capabilities and functionings have been proposed within the human development and capability literature. Yet, we need to take a step back and ask by which criteria they should be evaluated. That is, what criteria should a method for the selection of capabilities and functionings satisfy in order to be suitable for the task of setting a development agenda? In the next section, I discuss Robeyns's (2003, 70–1) five criteria and argue that they need further modification in order to be applicable for the present purpose of setting a development agenda.

5.2 Robeyns's Five Criteria for the Selection of Capabilities

What criteria should we use when selecting capabilities and functionings? Robeyns (2003, 70–1) has proposed one of the most influential sets of criteria within the capability literature, which has been employed to both empirical and theoretical purposes, including by Biggeri et al. (2006), Burchardt and Vizard (2011), Di Tommaso (2007), Gilroy (2007), and Walker (2006).

While Robeyns's criteria provide a good starting point for the evaluation of the different methods for the selection of capabilities, it has one shortcoming relative to our present purpose. The criteria suggested concern the selection of capabilities *for the analysis of gender inequalities within societies*. In the present context, however, we are interested in the selection of capabilities and functionings for *development purposes*. We should therefore ask whether or to what extent Robeyns's five criteria are suitable for this particular purpose.

There are two aspects to this. First, to what extent are the five criteria *necessary* when applied to the selection of capabilities relevant for addressing human development issues? That is, to what extent does each criteria for the selection of capabilities in general also apply by necessity to the selection of capabilities for human development purposes? Second, to what extent are the five criteria—by themselves or taken together—*adequate* for capturing what is at stake when selecting capabilities in the context of human development? On the one hand, is each criterion *by itself* adequately formulated to address human development? On the other hand, are the five criteria *taken together* adequate for addressing human development such that we do not need any further criteria?

To anticipate, I shall argue that while all five of Robeyns's criteria play some role in the context of human development, they do not fully capture what is at stake within discussions on human development. In the following I shall discuss each of Robeyns's criteria in turn and suggest what they add to the discussion on selecting capabilities relevant for development and where they fall short.

The first criterion identified by Robeyns is the idea that the list of capabilities and functionings "should be explicit, discussed, and defended" (Robeyns 2003, 70). As she argues, this may seem obvious within normative political philosophy but is not common practice within other disciplines, such as welfare economics where "functionings can be found in the available data sets, without defending an *a priori* list" (Robeyns 2003, 70). However, in absence of a proper discussion and defense, the particular list risks becoming contingent on readily available data and, from a normative philosophical perspective, arbitrarily excluding capabilities and functionings, which cannot be empirically measured.

What Robeyns's first criterion implies is that a list can only gain normative legitimacy if it is explicitly discussed and defended. Applied to the task of selecting capabilities and functionings for development purposes, then, the criterion of explicit formulation is necessary in order to normatively legitimize the consequent list. Human development is a development *ethics*; it aims to provide normative guidance to policy-makers and development practitioners. As a consequence, it is essential that a particular list of capabilities and functionings can be normatively legitimized and by extension, as Robeyns correctly argues, that the normative assumptions of the method of selection can be discussed and defended in an explicit manner.

To what extent is the criterion of explicit formulation adequately defined to suit the present purpose? Applied to the context of selecting capabilities for human development, we need to consider two issues with Robeyns's definition of the first criterion. First of all, she does not herself explicitly define what the standards of explicit formulation are. This is problematic, because without an adequate definition of the standards of explicit formulation it becomes impossible to judge when a particular method satisfies the criterion. Thus, in order to adequately define the criterion of explicit formulation it becomes imperative to define these standards.

By extension, second, the standards for explicit formulation may differ between disciplines. For example, the standards for anthropological empirical analysis differ not only from quantitative empirical studies (e.g., sociology) but also from the standards of philosophical analysis. Whereas normative political philosophy is primarily concerned about making the normative assumptions explicit, anthropological standards may focus on observational neutrality and descriptive thickness. Applied to the selection of capabilities and functionings relevant for human development, then, we should extend Robeyns's criterion of explicit formulation in two ways: an adequate method for the selection of capabilities should make both its normative assumptions explicit and consider the standards of explicitness within related disciplines.

The second criterion, identified by Robeyns, states that the particular method for the selection of capabilities should be justified, both in general and especially within the context of its application. The criterion of methodological justification builds on Robeyns's first criterion: the explicit formulation of normative assumptions allows us to scrutinize how the method is justified and the extent to which it is appropriate for the particular application.

This process of scrutinization and justification is necessary in order to avoid an arbitrary selection procedure; it is necessary because we need to know how and to what extent the proposed method is actually appropriate for the purpose. Consider, for example, the difference between identifying a list of capabilities, which a group of agents *actually* values, in contrast to identifying the capabilities they *ought* to value. The former is a descriptive question appropriate for an empirical method, while the latter is a normative question that arguably requires normative philosophical reasoning. Conversely, either method would be highly inappropriate (or, at the very least, inadequate) for addressing the opposite question. A method for the identification of capabilities and functionings relevant for setting a development agenda must likewise include a justification of why and how it is appropriate for this task.

The criterion of methodological justification is inadequately defined for this purpose, however. We can identify two issues, which a more specific criterion ought to address. First of all, the criterion must specify that the necessary justification should concern how the particular method is appropriate for the particular purpose. In this case, the methodological criterion should demand that the particular method can show how it is appropriate for selecting capabilities and functionings relevant for human development.

A second issue can be derived from this specification: Robeyns's definition—naturally, given her particular focus—does not clarify what kind of justification is necessary in order to show that a particular method is appropriate for the selection of capabilities within the domain of human development. We can identify at least three particular kinds of justification, which we may want a particular method to supply. To begin, we may want a *functional justification*. There are two aspects to this. On the one hand, a functional justification requires that a method can show that it is appropriate for the particular application—that is, that it includes an empirical function if applied to a descriptive task. On the other hand, a functional justification concerns the extent to which the method is practically feasible and reliable. For example, a method that aims to identify people's values by telepathically accessing their innermost thoughts would hardly be functionally justified unless it can be shown that such technology is available and reliable.

We may further distinguish between two other kinds of justifications, which concerns the particular tasks—normative and/or descriptive—required to identify a list of capabilities. As I argued earlier, different methods may be required to fulfill different tasks: while an empirical method may be best suited to identify the capabilities people have or would like to have, a normative philosophical method may be required for the identification of capabilities that people ought to (want to) have. In either case there are different standards of justification. A *philosophical justification* may require that the method adheres to and undergoes a process of philosophical rigor when specifying a list of capabilities. To what extent a method should be philosophically sound, however, may be up for debate. It is plausible, for example, that the imposition of philosophical standards of justification may prove excessive insofar as it stifles important nonphilosophical opinions (Argenton and Rossi 2013; Byskov 2017a). An *empirical justification*, meanwhile, may hold that a method should fulfill certain standards of qualitative and/or quantitative empirical analysis. A method for the selection of capabilities and functionings relevant for a development agenda should arguably provide all three kinds of justification to some degree.

The third criterion identified by Robeyns holds that the language, which the method uses, should be sensitive to the context of application. In other words, the particular list should be intelligible to the people who are meant to utilize the list, for example, policy-makers, moral philosophers, or development practitioners. While I agree that a suitable method for the selection of capabilities should be sensitive to context, Robeyns's definition coincides with the previous two criteria, which hold that a method, and how it formulates its list of capabilities, is subject to certain standards within the particular domains and disciplines to which it is applied.

Instead I propose that the criterion of contextual sensitivity encompasses two additional meanings. First, the purpose of making the list of capabilities intelligible is to make it practically applicable. Thus, to rephrase the criterion, a suitable method should be able to specify the list of capabilities such that it is applicable in practice, relative to the particular domain or discipline of application. Second, the idea of contextuality does not merely concern making the finished list intelligible. Rather, in selecting a list of capabilities, a method should be sensitive to the circumstances surrounding its context of application. Applied to human development, this becomes evident. Human development issues arise as a consequence of certain unfavorable socioeconomic and environmental circumstances. A method that ignores these contextual circumstances risks concocting a list of capabilities, which is unusable in practice, either because it does not address the specific problems or because it sets out unrealistic goals.

Robeyns's fourth criterion holds that the method should be able to be applied at different levels of generality. By 'levels of generality,' Robeyns (2003, 70) seems to imply that a list of capabilities can be specified at more or less abstract levels:

> For example, in philosophical discussions the list will be specified at a highly abstract level, whereas for political, social, or economic discussions the level of abstraction will be less abstract. And even within the latter discussions the level of abstraction can vary: the context of legal rights will require a list at a higher level of abstraction than one measuring socioeconomic inequality.

The criterion of different levels of generality should also be imposed on a method for the selection of capabilities relevant for a development agenda. For example, a list of basic and universal capabilities will necessarily be more abstract than a list of capabilities tailored to a specific community.

However, the taxonomy proposed by Robeyns is rather crude and, especially within the context of development, we should require a suitable method to similarly work at other levels of generality. First of all, within the human development domain we should demand that a suitable method for the selection of capabilities work at different levels of *geographical generality*. That is, a list of capabilities may apply globally, regionally, nationally, and locally. Likewise, a list of capabilities may apply to different levels of *demographical generality*. It may, for example, apply to all human beings (and maybe even animals) across time and space or to a particular subset of humans, such as women, children, or the disabled. Of course, the geographical and demographical levels of generality may overlap when the list applies to all members of a specific geographically defined community (e.g., all inhabitants of South Africa). A third level of generality, which is especially (but not exclusively) relevant for human development, concerns the institutional level at which the list is meant to be implemented. For example, it is reasonable to expect that a list of capabilities setting out the global development goals for the following decade will differ quite drastically from a list of capabilities utilized by an NGO focused on housing development in a rural village.

The fifth and final criterion that Robeyns proposes holds that the method should be able to identify all relevant capabilities and functionings within that domain of application. There are two aspects to this criterion. First, the list of capabilities should be specified such that it does not exclude any important elements relative to the application. As I take it, this means that a list of capabilities relevant for secondary education, for example, must include the capabilities for primary and secondary education but may be justified in excluding post-secondary levels of education, such as tertiary education and vocational training. The second aspect highlights that no important elements can be reduced to or subsumed under another capability. For example, if secondary education is the focus, the capabilities necessary for secondary education—for example, literacy, reasoning skills, access to transportation—cannot merely be subsumed or reduced to the more general capability for secondary education.

While I am sympathetic to Robeyns's need to specify the criterion of exhaustion and nonreduction categorically, we should recognize that selecting capabilities and functionings within a development context is a messy business. Especially two factors impose restrictions on the extent to which a method can satisfy this criterion. First, of all, it is not easy to identify the root causes of human development deprivations. As capability theorists have argued, poverty is a multidimensional concept, which is brought about by a multitude of circumstances (Alkire and Foster 2011). While a suitable method should naturally attempt to penetrate and illuminate these causes, we must admit that it is not always possible due to various constraints, such as a lack of budget, time, or data.

Second, there are a lot of different interests at stake within human development. Donor countries, for example, may primarily have an interest in seeing the inhabitants of developing nations grow out of their aid-dependency. As such, it is reasonable to expect that they would favor a list of capabilities that—directly or indirectly—support economic growth and independence. Other development agents, however, may have different interests, such as the fulfillment of basic needs or the stabilization of democratic institutions—ends which may not see them immediately be lifted out of their economic aid-dependency. In light of this, I propose to rephrase the criterion to include the idea that a suitable method should be able to identify all relevant capabilities *within its restrictions*. It should be noted that this is not meant as a rejection of the need for a method to be exhaustive, but rather to further specify the criterion to explicitly take these obstacles into account.

In sum, while Robeyns's five criteria provide a useful starting point, selecting capabilities and functionings relevant for human development is no easy task. The domain of human development is rife with complexity and nuances, and my analysis in this section shows that Robeyns's criteria require modifications in order to make them relevant for the particular purpose of setting a development agenda. In the following sections I shall propose four general criteria—methodological justification, normative justification, democratic legitimacy, and contextual sensitivity—which can constitute the considerations that were raised in the discussion of her criteria. An overview of the four criteria and their sub-clauses can be found in Table 5.1.

Table 5.1 Overview of the Four General Criteria, and Their Sub-clauses, That a Suitable Method for the Selection of Normatively Relevant Capabilities and Functionings for a Human Development Agenda Should Be Able to Satisfy

Criteria	*Methodological Justification*	*Normative Justification*	*Democratic Legitimacy*	*Contextual Sensitivity*
Definition	*A suitable method should be justifiable within the norms and standards of its methodological discipline(s).*	*A suitable method should be able to justify its methodology and its list of capabilities and functionings according to its chosen normative theory.*	*A suitable method should be sensitive to the will of the people to whom it applies—whether procedurally or in substance—and not impose its list on them.*	*A suitable method should be sensitive to local and nonideal sociocultural, economic, and environmental circumstances and conditions.*
Sub-clauses	Explicit formulation and scrutiny Feasibility and reliability Suitability for purpose	Explicit formulation and scrutiny Suitability for purpose Comprehensive outcome justification	Procedural inclusion and nondomination Different levels of application Concern for epistemic correctness	Different levels of application and abstraction Sensitivity to nonideal circumstances Revisability

5.3 Criterion of Methodological Justification

In my discussion of Robeyns's first two criteria—explicit formulation and methodological justification—I argued that they conflate two different concerns, namely the extent to which a method is justifiable (a) within its own methodological discipline and (b) in relation to a particular normative theory. Consider, for example, how the standards for anthropological empirical analysis differ not only from quantitative empirical studies (e.g., sociology), but also from the standards of philosophical analysis. An anthropological study may be valid insofar as it satisfies certain anthropological standards, such as neutrality and descriptive thickness, yet be invalid on a normative account insofar as its list of capabilities does not satisfy basic principles of justice. Thus, we should make a distinction between the extent to which a method satisfies the norms and standards of its chosen methodological discipline and the extent to which it satisfies basic normative principles.[3] The first criterion (see Table 5.2), discussed in the present section, focuses on methodological justification,

Table 5.2 The Criterion of Methodological Justification and Its Sub-clauses

Criterion of Methodological Justification			
A suitable method should be justifiable within the norms and standards of its methodological discipline(s)			
Sub-clause	Explicit formulation and scrutiny	Feasibility and reliability	Suitability for purpose
Definition	*A suitable method should make its normative and descriptive assumptions, its empirical data, and argumentation explicit to the extent that it can be subjected to scrutiny.*	*A suitable method should be both practically feasible and reliable.*	*A suitable method should be able to justify how and why it is suitable for the specific purpose.*

while the second criterion (see Table 5.3), relegated to the following section, focuses on the issue of normative justification.

The first criterion, I propose, states that *a suitable method should be justifiable within the norms and standards of its methodological discipline(s)*. In other words, the first criterion is necessary in order to ensure that the proposed method and its subsequent list of capabilities satisfy standards of scientific rigor. For example, selecting capabilities through quantitative analysis would require a statistically representative data set in order to conclude that relevant or valuable capabilities or functionings can be derived from it. Deriving relevant capabilities through qualitative analysis, however, requires the method to adhere to standards within ethnographic and anthropological research, such as observational neutrality and adequate descriptive depth (i.e., gathering of believable testimonies).

There are two aspects to this. First of all, as Robeyns points out, a suitable method should make its methodology explicit in order for it to be scrutinized. This includes specifying its normative and descriptive assumptions (if any; empirical sciences—often wrongly—claim to be normatively neutral), making its empirical basis available, and showing how a list of capabilities and functionings is explicitly derived from these inputs. We can refer to this as the sub-clause of *explicit formulation and scrutiny*. The sub-clause of explicit formulation and scrutiny is important in order to assess the second aspect of the criterion, namely the method's *feasibility and reliability*. As I argued earlier, the sub-clause of feasibility

Table 5.3 The Criterion of Normative Justification and Its Sub-clauses

Criterion of Normative Justification			
A suitable method should be able to justify its methodology and its list of capabilities and functionings according to its chosen normative theory.			
Sub-clause	Explicit formulation and scrutiny	Suitability for purpose	Comprehensive outcome justification
Definition	*A suitable method should make its normative assumptions explicit to the extent that they can be subjected to scrutiny.*	*A suitable method should be able to justify how and why its normative principles are suitable for the specific purpose.*	*A suitable method should provide a normative justification of both the procedure and the outcome.*

and reliability concerns the extent to which the method can be said to be practically applicable. Recall that a method that aims to identify people's values by telepathically accessing their innermost thoughts would hardly be functionally justified unless it can be shown that such technology is available and reliable.

Now, arguably, whenever we want to make a selection of capabilities and functionings we want our method to satisfy these two aspects—explicit formulation and scrutiny on the one hand, and feasibility and reliability on the other. As such, the two sub-clauses apply to the selection of capabilities and functionings in general. In this thesis, however, I am interested in specifying a method that can help us identify the normatively relevant capabilities and functionings for a human development agenda. Thus, we should add a third sub-clause to the criterion of methodological justification: a suitable method should be able to justify why this particular methodology is especially appropriate for the setting of a development agenda.

In sum, the criterion of methodological justification holds that it is necessary to make the methodology used explicit and scrutinize it according to the standards of the relevant methodological discipline(s). The criterion is needed in order to ensure that a list of capabilities and functionings is derived through or by means of a methodologically sound procedure—that the list follows from and is in accordance with the empirical evidence and/or theoretical argumentation—and that the method is actually suitable for the purpose to which it is applied.

5.4 Criterion of Normative Justification

A normative justification demands that the method and its list of capabilities and functionings can be at least minimally justified according to normative standards. That is, while the method and its list of capabilities should hold up to philosophical rigor in general, it is imperative that the selection procedure, as well as the items on the list of capabilities, do not violate basic normative principles, however specified and justified.

There are two aspects to a normative justification. First, a suitable method should make explicit what normative assumptions the selection of capabilities is grounded on. Does it rely on a specific conception of the human being? Does it assume ideal circumstances, such as rationality? Does it hold specific (controversial) normative or ontological views, such as individualism, communitarianism, atomism, or holism? Because the particular selection of capabilities will rely on these assumptions—consider, for example, how an individualist method might stress individual property rights—a suitable method must be able to provide a normative justification for these assumptions and thus for the particular capabilities and functionings on its list. Second, a suitable method should be able to justify why this exact normative grounding is especially appropriate for the purpose of selecting capabilities relevant for a development agenda. That is, it needs to show, on the one hand, how it can address development issues while, on the other hand, respecting the criteria outlined in this chapter. As above, these two sub-clauses are necessary in order to scrutinize and evaluate the method in question; a method, which does not make these aspects—that is, its normative assumptions and how it suits the specific purpose—explicit cannot be properly evaluated because we do not have access to the necessary information that allows us to perform this evaluation.

Yet such transparency is important because the normative assumptions of a particular method will affect both the procedure of selection as well as its outcome. Consider, for example, how an economic growth paradigm will affect both the procedure and the outcome of a selection of capabilities. Procedurally, this view would have good arguments for primarily extending decision-making and expert authority to economists and business developers rather than, for example, moral philosophers. In terms of outcome, a method that focuses on the creation of economic wealth will also likely prioritize capabilities and functionings that are conducive to the creation of economic wealth. For the evaluation of this method it is a crucial piece of information that it is committed to the normative assumption that economic growth holds the key to development—an assumption that is deeply contested.

It may be argued that only the outcome of the method (i.e., the particular list of capabilities and functionings), and not the procedure, needs to be normatively justifiable. That is, the proponents of this view hold, whether the procedure is just as irrelevant as long as it arrives at a normatively justifiable outcome. This view echoes Sen's (1997) distinction between the *culmination outcome* and the *comprehensive outcome* of a list of capabilities. While the culmination outcome only takes into consideration whether the final list of capabilities can be justified—that is, none of the items on the list violates principles of justice—the comprehensive outcome also considers the justifiability of the procedure by which the list was brought about. As many proponents of empowerment and indigenous knowledge argue, *how* we select certain capabilities for a development agenda is normatively important in at least one respect, namely the extent to which the procedure allows for the involvement of local stakeholders (Sillitoe 2004; Watene and Yap 2015). Hence, the normative justification should concern the comprehensive outcome and not merely the culmination outcome.

Does this mean that anything goes? Should a development agenda not respect basic normative principles? Of course it should. What is argued, however, is that such basic normative principles must be made explicit and be adequately scrutinized as part of the decision-making process before they can be imposed on a particular selection of capabilities and functionings. As such, the formulation of the basic normative principles that a development agenda should respect is part of the method itself and not something that can or should be specified in advance.

In sum, the second criterion that we should impose on a method for the selection of capabilities and functionings relevant for a development agenda holds that the method should be able to provide a minimal normative justification for its choice of procedure and of the items on its list of capabilities and functionings. That is, a suitable method should be able to specify and justify why a particular selection procedure is relevant for setting a development agenda and how each capability and functioning on the agenda is relevant for addressing development issues. In particular, I have argued that the method needs to respect at least the three normative views that I have set out so far in this thesis.

5.5 Criterion of Democratic Legitimacy

In the previous section I noted that many (capability) theorists have argued for granting local stakeholders more authority in deciding on matters of development. In extending such authority, we should say that the method (and its subsequent list of capabilities) gains *democratic legitimacy*. The criterion of democratic legitimacy (see Table 5.4) is the claim that a suitable method for the selection of capabilities should be able to represent the values and preferences of the people to whom the list of capabilities applies by including them in the socioscientific and political decision-making process.

A concern for democratic legitimacy implies a concern with the *procedure* by which a list of capabilities is selected as stated by Sen's (1997) notion of comprehensive outcome (see above) and especially Jaggar (2006) and Robeyns (2005) have argued that those to whom a list of capabilities applies should be included in the selection procedure so as not to impose the list on them. Thus, a democratically legitimate procedure of selection should allow the people, to whom the consequent list of

Table 5.4 The Criterion of Democratic Legitimacy and Its Sub-clauses

Criterion of Democratic Legitimacy			
A suitable method should be sensitive to the will of the people to whom it applies—whether procedurally or in substance—and not impose its list on them.			
Sub-clause	Procedural inclusion and nondomination	Different levels of application	Concern for epistemic correctness
Definition	*A suitable method should include local stakeholders in the decision-making process and not impose a development agenda on them against their will.*	*A suitable method should be democratically legitimate at all stages and levels of application.*	*A suitable method should weigh democratic legitimacy against a concern for epistemic correctness.*

capabilities will apply, to influence, discuss, criticize, object to, and refute both the procedure as well as the selection of capabilities.

However, there may be epistemic reasons for limiting democratic participation in the selection of capabilities: in some regards, more democratic participation leads to worse decisions. This may be, for example, when the public suffers from adaptive preferences or when they have little insight into some of the more technical aspects of development. A concern for epistemic correctness is not a sufficient reason for excluding local stakeholders completely from the selection procedure, however. As proponents of indigenous knowledge stress, local stakeholders may likewise possess tacit, embodied, and experiential knowledge about the local circumstances that external development experts do not have access to, which needs to be complimented with the more technical knowledge of traditional development experts (DeWalt 1994).

In sum, this discussion reveals three sub-clauses to the criterion of democratic legitimacy (see Table 5.4). First, the criterion of democratic legitimacy demands that local stakeholders are able to participate in the selection procedure and that the list of capabilities is not imposed on them against their will. Second, authority should be extended to local stakeholders at all levels and stages of the method's application (i.e., within both the political and socioscientific domains). Third, democratic legitimacy should be weighed against a concern for epistemic correctness.

5.6 Criterion of Contextual Sensitivity

Human development is concerned with both those capabilities and functionings that are relevant for all human beings at any time or place as well as those, the lack of which, may be said to constitute a human development deprivation relative to a particular socioeconomic context. Consequentially, a suitable method must be able to adjust the context and its scope according to whether the selection of capabilities is being applied at a global, regional, national, or local level (see Table 5.5).

As Vandemoortele (2012, 29) argues, a list of capabilities and functionings on a global level neither can nor should be exhaustive in terms of reflecting what is relevant for human development. A global list of capabilities, rather, should aim to capture those capabilities (and functionings) that can be said to be universally valued. More locally applied lists of capabilities, to the contrary, can and should depart from the global lists for two reasons. First, whereas a global list is purposely left unspecific, a local list must capture the particular issue(s) at stake. Thus, second, a selection of capabilities needs to be tailored to the specific socioeconomic circumstances. Consequently, the first sub-clause should specify that a method for the selection of capabilities relevant for addressing human development issues must recognize that human development takes place both at the global as well as on regional, national, and local levels.

Why do we need a method to be contextually sensitive? The short answer is that this sensitivity is instrumental in justifying how the method is able to correctly identify what is at stake within human development. Consider, for example, how many of the failures of development can be ascribed to a lack of understanding of the issues at stake (e.g., Ferguson 1990, 1994). The first thing we should notice is that, descriptively speaking, the conditions surrounding human development are decidedly nonideal and not always visible to those unfamiliar with the local context. They exist in a space of social norms, cultural traditions, economic

Table 5.5 The Criterion of Contextual Sensitivity and Its Sub-clauses

Criterion of contextual sensitivity			
A suitable method should be sensitive to local and non-ideal sociocultural, economic, and environmental circumstances and conditions.			
Sub-clause	Different levels of abstraction and application	Revisability	Sensitivity to non-ideal circumstances
Definition	*A suitable method should be able to specify a list of capabilities and functionings at different levels of abstraction that suit different levels of application*	*A suitable method should be able to revise its list of capabilities and functionings in light of new and better evidence, reasons, and arguments*	*A suitable method should be sensitive to the non-ideal circumstances surrounding human development*

inequalities, limited resources and other contingencies. When designing development policies and programs, then, development scholars and practitioners must often work from assumptions about how the concrete development intervention will affect the state of affairs. This requires great knowledge and understanding of the social and economic context in which the development intervention will take place.

Taking contextual conditions into consideration presents us with the following issue: contextual conditions may constrain what it is feasible to achieve with a development agenda. To what extent should a method for the selection of capabilities for a development agenda take such *feasibility constraints* into concern? On the one hand, there are benefits to not taking feasibility constraints into consideration. For example, as Valentini (2012, 659)[4] argues, "the more factual constraints are introduced in the elaboration of normative principles, the more these will appear to offer an uncritical defence of the *status quo*." We need to specify an ideal state of justice that does not take facts into consideration in order to be able to evaluate and criticize the status quo (Cohen 2003).

The problem with an idealized list, however, is that it unpractical for addressing human development issues (Robeyns 2008; Valentini 2012, 659). That is, the purpose of a list of capabilities is not primarily to *evaluate* the status quo, but rather to provide a *prescriptive* theory for how we can address real life human development issues (although the specification of an idealized list of capabilities may be a step in defining a practically applicable list). Because human development issues exist in a reality of nonideal circumstances, an agenda that can be applied to address these issues must take account of the constraints that prevent the realization of an idealized list. The second sub-clause should thus specify that contextual sensitivity implies taking nonideal circumstances into consideration in this way.

As noted earlier, a list of capabilities does not merely aim to *describe* human development, however. Just as importantly, the purpose of specifying such a list is to provide a normative *prescription* to various development actors, such as global development institutions, national governments, and NGOs, about what *ought* to be secured or promoted by development policies, interventions, and projects. This means that the mere fact that human development takes place in a nonideal space does not entail that the prescriptive list cannot assume ideal circumstances.

Should our method specify the ideal society or, conversely, focus on how we can improve from the current state of affairs without necessarily determining an ideal society? While especially Sen (2006b, 2009) has argued that an end-state theory is neither necessary nor sufficient for determining improvements in justice or, in our case, development (Valentini 2012, 661), several scholars have argued that we need to know what an ideal state of justice or development looks like in order to determine just how unjust or underdeveloped the status quo is and thus how to improve on it (Gilabert 2011; Robeyns 2012; Valentini 2011; Stemplowska 2008). In this regard, specifying an ideal end-state for development becomes *part of* specifying a nonideal, transitional theory for the improvement of development. Let us therefore specify the third subclause in the following way: a suitable method should make its list of capabilities and functionings open to revisions in light of better empirical evidence and/or better normative reasons and arguments.

In sum, while an ideal list of capabilities may be more justifiable in relation to normative theory, it is hardly implementable insofar as it specifies capabilities, which are unattainable in practice (at least for the time being). Hence, I have argued that a development agenda should be sensitive to contextual circumstances, including feasibility constraints. The extent to which a development agenda must represent local contextual conditions, however, depends on its level of application. Whereas a local development agenda should be highly sensitive to the socioeconomic context, a global development agenda can allow itself to be more abstract. Finally, I have argued that although a development agenda should be contextually sensitive, it should likewise be sensitive to revisions in light of normative arguments and empirical evidence.

5.7 Concluding Remarks

In this chapter I have argued that we should evaluate the proposed methods for the selection of capabilities and functionings according to four general criteria: the criterion of methodological justification holds that a suitable method should satisfy the norms of its methodological discipline(s); the criterion of normative justification states that a suitable method should make its normative assumptions explicit and provide normative justification of its list of capabilities; the criterion of democratic legitimacy states that a suitable method should include local stakeholders in the decision-making process; and the criterion of contextual sensitivity holds that a development agenda should be sensitive to nonideal socioeconomic conditions, while remaining open to revisions in light of better normative arguments and empirical evidence. With this list of criteria in hand, in the next chapter I evaluate fifteen distinct methods for the selection of capabilities and functionings proposed within the capability literature.

Notes

1 Both well-being and agency can further be conceived of in terms of achievements.
2 See Sen (1985, 204–8) for an expansion on the relationship between well-being freedom and agency freedom.
3 Of course, these two concerns will tend to overlap if the chosen method makes use of normative philosophical reasoning.
4 For similar arguments, see Stemplowska (2008, 332–3) and Robeyns (2008).

6 Methods for the Selection of Capabilities and Functionings

Several methods for the selection of capabilities and functionings have been proposed within the capability literature. Which method should we prefer when selecting capabilities and functionings that are normatively relevant for development? In this chapter, fifteen proposed methods, categorized as ad hoc, foundational, procedural, and mixed (or multi-stage) methods, are identified and discussed.[1] Ad hoc methods base their selection of capabilities on pragmatic considerations, foundational methods on some ultimate normative value or principle, procedural methods on more open-ended, democratic information, while mixed (or multi-stage) methods employ two or more foundational and procedural methods in conjunction.

It is argued that selecting capabilities and functionings relevant for human development requires a mixed (or multi-stage) method. Ad hoc methods are dismissed because of their lack of methodological and normative justification, foundational methods due to a lack of democratic legitimacy and contextual sensitivity, while procedural methods are found vulnerable to implicit biases and adaptive preferences. Mixed (or multi-stage) methods, however, can provide both methodological and normative justifications as well as provide democratic legitimacy and contextual sensitivity.

The chapter adds to the capability literature in two ways. First, it provides an up-to-date systematic and comprehensive discussion of the many distinct methods for the selection of capabilities and functionings found within the capability literature.[2] Second, it identifies key advantages of and concerns with the different methods. The chapter thus answers an important question: by which method should we select normatively relevant capabilities and functionings for development purposes?

The chapter is structured as follows. Before the identified methods are discussed, the first section (6.1) introduces and discusses a persistent disagreement between capability scholars interested in the selection of relevant capabilities, namely whether it is a philosophical or a democratic task. It is argued that the binary distinction between the democratic and philosophical positions is too simple to capture the diversity of methods by which capability scholars have attempted to sketch a list of relevant capabilities. The following four sections (6.2–6.5) introduce, analyze, and discuss the four general methodological categories—ad hoc, foundational, procedural, and mixed (or multi-stage) methods—as well as their more specific methods in turn. From this discussion, it is concluded that the multi-stage method, which I label the *synthesizing method*, is best suited to the task selecting normatively relevant capabilities and functionings because it can integrate theoretical and empirical, technical and procedural, insights alike. In section 6.6 I finally investigate whether and the extent to which synthesizing methods for the selection of capabilities are compatible with the claims and commitments that I have made in the previous chapter of this book.

6.1 Philosophical, Democratic, and Practical Concerns in Selecting Capabilities

The capability literature has traditionally presented the issue of selecting relevant or valuable capabilities as a disagreement between those who hold that it is a public task and those who argue that some essential capabilities can and should be selected by normative philosophers. While the former, procedural or democratic position has commonly been associated with Sen, the latter, philosophical position is often attributed to Nussbaum and her followers (Byskov 2017a 3).

Although it is true that the methods for the selection of relevant capabilities can be more or less democratic and more or less philosophical, this binary distinction between the democratic and philosophical positions is too simple to capture the diversity of methods by which capability scholars have attempted to sketch a list of relevant capabilities. Ballon (2013, 7), for example, identifies three general methods used in the empirical capability literature: normative views, quantitative methods, and especially designed surveys. *Normative views* base their selection of capabilities either ad hoc on the values of the researcher or on moral theory (e.g., a theory of justice). *Quantitative methods* extract relevant capabilities from statistical data, either by summarizing the information in the original data set or by confirming them through further quantitative analysis. Finally, *especially designed surveys* gather information about relevant and valuable capabilities through qualitative studies, often with a specific purpose. Other methods recognized in the literature include democratic deliberation and participatory exercises (Burchardt and Vizard 2011, 95).

Whereas Ballon (2013) merely surveys and categorizes some of the empirical capability literature, this chapter goes beyond Ballon's categories to analyze and discuss the *justification* of the proposed methods for the selection of capabilities. Before the various methods are discussed, however, three preliminary remarks should be made. First, it is important to note that the chapter will not provide a comprehensive survey of the empirical capability literature. In that respect, please refer to Ballon (2013) and Robeyns (2006) as good starting points. Rather, the following sections will be an amalgamation of the literature; examples of the various methods through references to empirical studies and practical uses where appropriate will of course be provided.

Second, not all of the identified methods are explicitly concerned with development and some are only secondarily concerned with the selection of capabilities. This, however, does not exclude the possibility that they may actually be appropriate for the selection of capabilities relevant for development purposes and thus warrant further scrutiny in this regard. While most of the identified methods are found to be question-begging when applied to selecting capabilities for development purposes, *it is by no means* intended to deny their applicability in other regards or that they may play a valuable part of a method for the selection of relevant capabilities for development or otherwise. In fact, the aim is to show that all of these methods may provide us with crucial insights for the selection of relevant capabilities for human development, although neither method is in itself *sufficient* for this purpose.[3]

Third, a list of capabilities can have different purposes. For example, a list of basic capabilities may be used to specify a capability theory of justice while the relative welfare of a society may be indicated by a list of functionings that its citizens have. A list of capabilities and functionings relevant for human development may have two main purposes. First, it can be used to *evaluate* existing human development policies and, second, to *develop* new ones. In the first case, the existing states of affairs and human development practices are interpreted and judged through the lens of a list of capabilities; in the latter case, the list of capabilities provides the normative requirement, which ought to be implemented in practice.

Without further ado, let me proceed to the analysis, categorization, and evaluation of the methods proposed within the capability literature. An overview of the methods can be found in Table 6.1. The fifteen identified methods are divided into four general methodological categories: ad hoc, foundational, procedural, and mixed (or multi-stage) methods.[4] We can characterize the four methodological categories in the following way:

- *Ad hoc methods* are characterized by their lack of methodological justification. These methods do not adhere to any normative theories, but rather base their selection of capabilities on ad hoc considerations, such as the purpose of the study, the researcher's own values, or practical and pragmatic concerns. For example, a welfare economist may simply take an existing data set, and base their selection on whatever functionings are included in that data set. The selection is then fully determined by the choice of the data set and the available functionings in the data set.

Table 6.1 Overview of Methods for the Selection of Capabilities and Functionings Proposed within the Human Development and Capability Literature

General methodology	*Description*	*Specific methods*		*Selected authors*
Ad hoc methods	Selection based on ad hoc considerations **Characteristics:** Provisional; contextual; pragmatic or intuitive justification	Purpose of study		
		Researcher's own values/normative views		Human Development Index (UNDP 2015), Sen (1985a, 1985b), Slottje (1991), Klasen (2000)
		Pragmatic concerns and practical issues		
Foundational methods	Normatively relevant capabilities and functionings are derived from normative values and principles **Characteristics:** Absolute; universal; theoretical justification	Deductive reasoning	Internalist essentialism	Early Nussbaum (1990, 1992), Qizilbash (1998)
			Dialectically necessary judgments	Claassen and Düwell (2013)
		Overlapping consensus		Later Nussbaum (2011b)
		Technical knowledge	Human rights theory	Vizard (2006, 2007, 2010), Fukuda-Parr (2011), Osmani (2005), Sengupta (2002)
			Others	
Procedural methods	Normatively relevant capabilities and functionings are contingent on the social, cultural, and political context **Characteristics:** Democratic; open-ended; contextual; empirical or discursive justification	Deliberative democracy		Anderson (1999, 2003), Crocker (2005, 2008), Drydyk (2005), Sen (1999, 2001, 2002), Sen and Scanlon (2004), Drèze and Sen (2002)
		Qualitative analysis	Narrative approaches	Hodgett and Deneulin (2009), Biggeri et al. (2006), Phelps (2006), Clark (2002), Clark (2005)
			Participatory approaches	Biggeri et al. (2006), Clark (2008), Frediani (2007), Doyal and Gough (1991)
		Quantitative analysis	Data-driven selection	Schokkaert and Ootgem (1990), Lelli (2001)
			Confirmatory methods	Kuklys (2005), Krishnakumar (2007), Comim (2008)
Mixed (or multi-stage) methods	Integrates two or more technocratic and procedural methods **Characteristics:** Holistic; dialectical; conflicting; both theoretical and empirical/discursive justification	Comparative methods		Brock (2009), Burchardt and Vizard (2011), Vizard (2010), Holland (2014a, 2014b)
		Synthesizing methods		Alkire (2002), Claassen (2011), Khader (2011)

- *Foundational methods* hold that a list of capabilities and functionings can be derived (solely) from some ultimate normative value or principle, such as human agency, human dignity, or human rights, which grounds the selection. As such, foundational lists tend to claim to be universally applicable, although the items on the lists may be further specified to suit local circumstances.
- *Procedural methods* derive a list of capabilities from an open-ended empirical or deliberative procedure. As such, these methods base the selection on people's (reasoned) subjective preferences. A list of capabilities is thus contingent on the social, cultural, and political context and is justified based on empirical findings and/or the political and deliberative discourse.
- *Mixed (or multi-stage) methods* combine one or more foundational method(s) with one or more procedural method(s). As such, mixed methods aim to integrate different sources of knowledge (e.g., normative theory, human rights theory, qualitative and quantitative analyses, democratic deliberations) to provide a dialectical and holistic approach.

In the following sections I analyze and discuss each general methodological category, and their more specific methods, in turn. It is shown that the first three methodologies—that is, ad hoc, foundational, and procedural methods—all have serious shortcomings when applied to the context of selecting capabilities and functionings for human development purposes.[5]

6.2 Ad hoc Methods

The first set of methods for the selection of capabilities distinguishes itself by its lack of methodological justification. That is, these methods base the selection of capabilities and functionings on ad hoc or pragmatic considerations, such as personal values, intuitions, or availability of data, and hence lack both robust normative and methodological justifications. Because these methods and their subsequent lists of capabilities lack normative and methodological justification, I shall not regard them as sufficiently justified to warrant further discussion other than to mention them in the name of completeness. We can distinguish three such methods. The first set of methods bases its selection of capabilities on the particular purpose of the study. The second uses the researcher's own values as the basis for the selection (Ballon 2013, 7; 9–10), while the third set selects capabilities out of pragmatic concerns, for example, a lack of reliable or available data on some capabilities (Hodgett and Deneulin 2009, 66).

First, the capability approach can be applied to many specific purposes and the relevant capabilities may vary between these different purposes. For example, we may want to investigate a rural community's access to clean drinking water. For such an investigation it stands to reason that some capabilities are more relevant than others. While access to clean water reservoirs, wells, and means of transportation are crucial capabilities in this context, other capabilities, such as having the freedom to be a mother or to be sheltered, are less important, although crucial in other respects. Restricting the selection of relevant capabilities in this way is entirely ad hoc and specific to the purpose. In doing so, the researcher fails to consider whether the capabilities in question are at all relevant to the specific community or whether they are normatively important (although, of course, the researcher may have a good intuition in both regards).

Second, Ballon (2013, 9) identifies a set of empirical studies in which the list of capabilities is based on the interests and/or values of the researcher. Again, the selection of capabilities here is made ad hoc because the researcher does not base it on any evidence of its normative importance for people's well-being and development (although, of course, the researcher may very well be right in her assumption). The Human Development Index (HDI) selection of capabilities (i.e., basic education, longevity, and income) may be seen as an example of such ad hoc selection process. Although the value of these three indicators has been defended in the Human Development Reports, the decision to restrict the number of capabilities was mainly a political one as it fostered clarity and brevity. Accordingly, the HDI has often been accused of providing an incomplete and superficial picture of human well-being and development.

Third, Hodgett and Deneulin (2009, 66) note that many researchers do not base their selection of capabilities on normative or practical reason, but rather on "pragmatic concerns of data availability." Because some capabilities are notoriously difficult to measure, they are often not considered by researchers. There are three reasons underlying researchers' omission of certain capabilities. First, there may be no data available on that particular capability and it may be difficult to obtain any due to it being difficult to measure for one reason or another (e.g., it could be a culturally sensitive subject). For example, data on domestic violence is not readily available and people are often adverse to open up about the subject. Thus, researchers may make the pragmatic decision to include other dimensions of gender equity while excluding domestic violence. Second, the available data may not be reliable or reflect reality. For example, the survey may not investigate all sources of information, while subjects may misrepresent or report false data. While omitting such incomplete or unreliable data might be valid, this decision is nonetheless based on pragmatic considerations. Finally, the researchers themselves may be vulnerable to cognitive biases that lead them to ignore certain otherwise relevant dimensions.

Thus, in sum, there may be a variety of pragmatic or practical reasons why capability scholars—especially empirical researchers—may choose to include or omit certain capabilities. These reasons, nevertheless, remain entirely ad hoc, as they are not based on considerations of the normative relevance or value of these capabilities. Ad hoc methods for the selection of relevant capabilities are inadequate and inappropriate exactly because they fail to consider the relevance and justification of its capabilities and functionings. A selection of capabilities for development purposes must be minimally justifiable, both as a matter of normative theory (Claassen 2011, 496; Nussbaum 2003, 47) or democratic legitimacy (Claassen 2011, 491; Jaggar 2006; Byskov 2017a 5; Robeyns 2005, 199). The following two sections thus discuss two general methodologies that aim to provide either a theoretical grounding or a procedural justification of a list of capabilities and functionings.

6.3 Foundational Methods

Methods belonging to the second category arrive at a list of capabilities and functionings through theoretical reasoning (as opposed to deriving it from empirical studies). As such, they all rely on generalized hypotheses about what is necessary for decent human life or a just state of affairs. We can identify three sets of foundational methods: deductive reasoning, overlapping consensus, and technical knowledge. In the following, each is discussed in turn.

The most prominent type of foundational method is *deductive reasoning*. Deductive reasoning is the idea that one starts out with a normative theory, which includes some ultimate and fundamental value(s) or principle(s), such as human dignity or agency, and then work backwards to identify the capabilities and functionings that are necessary for people to have in order to satisfy this normative theory. In other words, from what is morally desirable we can deduce a list of relevant capabilities. Especially the early Nussbaum (1990, 1992) uses a version of deductive reasoning, which she labels 'internalist essentialism.'

Nussbaum's *internalist essentialism* identifies human characteristics by asking us whether or not we agree with certain common sense judgments about human life. For example, does human life involve social relationships? Someone denying this common sense judgment faces a trilemma (Nussbaum 1995, 108–9). If she cannot convince everyone else of her conviction, she must either sever any ties with her friends and family and go live by herself, or she must contradict her own conviction that human life does not include social relationships. Nussbaum claims that it is implausible that people would be convinced that human life does not involve social relations and because the second option comes at such a high cost it is doubtful whether anyone would choose it. If these assumptions hold, Nussbaum argues, we should include the capability for social relations, such as holding friendships and participating in a community, on a list of essential characteristics of human life.[6]

Claassen and Düwell (2013) have recently criticized Nussbaum's method of internal essentialism. While sympathetic to Nussbaum's project of identifying essential capabilities through a process of deductive reasoning, Claassen and Düwell (2013) argue that insofar as the critic of Nussbaum's list is sufficiently willing to deny some of the items on the list, he is perfectly able to do so. For example, although Nussbaum includes the capability for humor on her list, while omitting the capability for aggression, it is perfectly conceivable that someone may live an aggressive life without humor and that "we have no reason to think that the costs of that person doing so are unbearably high" (Claassen and Düwell 2013, 500).

As an alternative to Nussbaum's method, Claassen and Düwell (2013) suggest that there are certain capabilities that any agent must necessarily accept insofar as she is an agent; something that would be self-contradictory to deny because the denial itself necessitates having this capability. Claassen and Düwell (2013, 501) find this argument in Gewirth (1978, 1996) concept of *dialectically necessary judgments*. Dialectically necessary judgments are the things we cannot deny on pain of self-contradiction (Claassen and Düwell 2013, 504–5).

The method of dialectically necessary judgments starts out from the claim that in order to make *any* moral judgments, it is dialectically necessary for us to value having the capability for agency because agency is a necessary condition for making moral judgments in the first place (Claassen and Düwell 2013, 504). From the claim that we recognize ourselves as agents, Gewirth argues that it is dialectically necessary for us to value the means for that enable us to exercise our agency, namely freedom and well-being, broadly defined (Claassen and Düwell 2013, 505). Accordingly, a list of capabilities and functionings should include the freedoms and the well-being necessary to exercise our agency.

However, there are many issues that are relevant for development, which do not concern the necessary means for agency and many questions can be answered both affirmatively and negatively without violating one's agency. Consider, for example, the issue of teen pregnancies, which is a big problem in low- and middle-income countries, according to WHO (2015). Should the capabilities for sexual education and contraception be a matter of development out of dialectical necessity? It is difficult to see how denying oneself the right to these capabilities is self-contradictory to the exercise of one's agency or that the generic features of one's agency—well-being and freedom—are thereby denied. It is perfectly consistent for someone to deny these capabilities without consequently having her agency, well-being, or freedom threatened. That is, the capabilities for sexual education and contraception are arguably not linked to one's capacity for making moral judgments and, hence, denying them would not (necessarily) amount to denying one's agency or the necessary means to exercise this agency.

Of course, it would be an entirely other matter if these rights were denied *by someone else* and whatever we think about development, it should not clash with the rights of all agents to well-being and freedom. But because the method of dialectical necessary judgments starts from what *oneself* as an agent, defined as the capacity to make moral judgments, can or cannot deny as a matter of self-contradiction, it remains indeterminate in cases where one does not deny one's agency or generic features thereof, namely well-being and freedom. While the example does not entail that the method of dialectically necessary judgments must remain entirely silent on these issues, it does imply that the method cannot by itself fulfill the role of selecting relevant capabilities for human development purposes.

Departing from her internalist essentialism, Nussbaum (2011b) has more recently justified her list of capabilities, following Rawls, by relying on an *overlapping consensus*. The method of overlapping consensus proceeds by identifying the capabilities and functionings, which different ethical systems can agree to. As an example, religious freedom can be subject to an overlapping consensus among different religious ethical systems insofar as they all want the freedom to practice their religious beliefs, although they disagree on many other issues.

Barclay (2003), Ferracioli and Terlazzo (2014), and Robeyns (2016), however, have argued that several of the items on Nussbaum's list cannot be subject to an overlapping consensus. For example, as Robeyns (2016, 14–15) argues, it is difficult to envision how pro-choice and pro-life activists could ever come to an overlapping consensus on the issue of having the capability to abortion, which is contained under the capability of bodily integrity on Nussbaum's list (Dixon et al. 2011). Nussbaum's list of capabilities, Robeyns concludes, is not only controversial with regard to some of the items on the list, it will also be quite limited in terms of which capabilities we can actually reach an overlapping consensus on.

Nussbaum could respond, however, that the objection is based on the empirical fact that different agents disagree on one particular item on her list, *not* on whether, given adequate normative arguments and reasons, a group of reasonable deliberators would be able to arrive at an overlapping consensus on *some* list of central capabilities, possibly including the right to abortion. In other words, this response goes, Nussbaum's defense of abortion as a central capability is based on normative arguments and reasons that sufficiently reasonable agents can *hypothetically* agree to—come to an overlapping consensus on—and thus not on any assumption about what capabilities and functionings that are, empirically speaking, subjects of consensus.

In response, Robeyns (2016, 14) argues that even if we take the overlapping consensus to be between reasonable agents, the persistent disagreements within the philosophical literature on many issues of ethics in general and social justice in particular, including the right to abortion, support the conclusion that a list of central capabilities, arrived at through an overlapping consensus, would indeed be quite minimal at best or impossible at worst. It is often possible to invoke sound normative arguments and reasons in support of antagonistic positions.[7]

The last foundational method derives a list of capabilities and functionings from *technical knowledge*. Within the capability literature technical knowledge has especially been obtained from *human rights theory*. Here, a list of capabilities may be found in academic works as well as in international conventions and declarations on human rights (Vizard 2007, 234–5).[8] Human rights are entitlements a person has by virtue of being human and which other people and institutions in turn have an obligation to provide them with (Fukuda-Parr 2011, 75; Sengupta 2002, 843). Thus, in combining the capability approach with human rights theory, the proponents of a human rights-based capability framework hold that—similar to Claassen and Düwell (2013) and Nussbaum (2011a, 2011b)—we can identify some basic capabilities, which a person is entitled to in virtue of being human/a human agent and which must accordingly be fulfilled.

Can a human rights–based capability framework form the basis for the selection of capabilities relevant for development purposes? Human rights theory may certainly supplement the capability approach in many ways. As Vizard (2007, 227) argues, the capability approach is underspecified and incomplete and a human rights theory may help provide (a) "a theoretical basis for making judgments about the relative values of different capabilities" and (b) "adequate grounds for explaining how the elements of a subset of basic and central (or highly valuable) capabilities might be specified and justified." Moreover, whereas the question of obligation is largely ignored within the capability approach, human rights theory may provide an account of legal accountability (Fukuda-Parr 2011, 77–8; Vizard 2007, 248; Sengupta 2002, 843, 873).

Yet, as Fukuda-Parr (2011, 75) notes, human rights are usually not directly concerned with development issues. The main issue is that human rights are concerned with the basic capabilities we are entitled to as a matter of justice (Sengupta 2002, 845), whereas human development arguably concerns more than only justice. Vizard (2007, 245) admits these limitations: even if human rights can be extended to concern development issues, "[l]ists of basic capabilities derived from lists of internationally recognized [. . .] should be viewed as *minimal* lists generated by just one of the various background or supplementary theories and methods."

A more general issue with the foundational methods, including those building on technical knowledge, is that they are decidedly top-down: a list of normatively relevant capabilities and functionings is essentially decided at a theoretical level and then applied in practice. This top-down approach has been met with two objections, which we can refer to, respectively, as *the objection from democratic legitimacy* and *the objection from epistemology* (Claassen 2011, 491–4; Byskov 2017a, 5–6). The objection from democratic legitimacy holds that a technocratic list is illegitimate because it bypasses those who are meant to benefit from it (Claassen 2011, 491; Jaggar 2006; Byskov 2017a, 5; Robeyns 2005, 199). That is, "[i]f the people to whom the list will apply reasonably feel that it is imposed on them, then the list will lack the necessary legitimacy" (Robeyns 2005, 199) because "such lists should be the outcome of a democratic process, or a process of public reasoning" (Claassen 2011, 491). The objection from epistemology, on the other hand, holds that there are epistemological limits to what the theorist or development-expert can know about, which capabilities matter to citizens (Claassen 2011, 504; Byskov 2017a, 6). If this is so, then a list of capabilities will be incomplete in terms of substance. For a list of capabilities to adequately address concerns for democratic legitimacy and epistemic correctness, it must be arrived at through a process in which local stakeholders have had the authority and opportunity to influence the outcome.

Proponents of the foundational methods could argue that the two issues of epistemology and democratic legitimacy can be avoided if we acknowledge that the normative theories, by which foundational methods derive a list of capabilities, implicitly rely on a discourse ethics. Discourse ethics is the idea that the normative validity of an argument—such as a proposed list of capabilities—can be derived from a reconstructive analysis of what counts as a normatively valid argument in everyday moral discourse. If foundational methods rely on a development ethics, this response goes, they can avoid the two objections—from democratic legitimacy and epistemology, respectively—because they actually derive their normative validity from a reconstructive analysis of deliberative practices and social norms.

Yet this response seems to be inadequate as a defense of foundational methods—defined as the proposition that a list of capabilities and functionings can be justified with reference to some ultimate normative principle or value—because they then also (implicitly) rely on procedural methods, such as empirical investigations, anthropological analyses, historical investigations, or democratic deliberations. If it is the case that foundational methods either implicitly or explicitly make use of such procedural methodology, we may want to categorize them as mixed (or multi-stage) methods, which integrate foundational and procedural methods.

This is not to say, however, that foundational methods cannot bring anything valuable to the discussion on development. Foundational methods can add a critical perspective based on normative values and principles to a discussion, which is vulnerable to moral relativism insofar as they also aim to include local perspectives and values. Thus, in sum, while foundational methods may be relevant for the identification of normatively relevant capabilities and functionings for human development, they are in themselves inadequate at fulfilling this task.

Moreover, we still need to investigate whether a foundational method is needed at all in this regard or whether a procedural method can provide such critical insight without grounding the selection of capabilities and functionings in an ultimate normative value or principle. Accordingly, the following section discusses the category of procedural methods.

6.4 Procedural Methods

There are a number of approaches that base a selection of capabilities more or less squarely on people's corrected or reasoned, yet subjective, beliefs, values, or preferences. Rather than making theoretical strides to identify capabilities based on an ultimate normative value or principle, the proponents of these methods base a selection of capabilities on investigations into the capabilities people value and/or need. In this sense, they rely on bottom-up (rather than top-down or theoretical) *procedural methods* to the selection of capabilities and functionings. At least three procedural methods can be identified. *Quantitative analyses* base their lists of capabilities on statistical data; *qualitative analyses* base them on in-depth inquiries into the reasons and preferences of selected groups of agents; and *deliberative democracy* selects capabilities based on the reasoned and expressed preferences of deliberators in democratic process.

Before we proceed to analyze and evaluate the three procedural methods, I need to address the concern that selecting capabilities and functionings through a pure procedural method is a nonstarter. Even procedural methods, this objection goes, rely on the normative view that a list of capabilities and functionings can only be justified with reference to people's actual values and preferences. If this is true, the objection concludes, it makes a purely procedural method impossible from the outset.

However, we need to distinguish between the justification of the method and the process of selecting capabilities and functionings. Although the procedural methods may need to rely on normative theories—such as discourse ethics or deliberative democratic theory—when justifying why we should prefer a procedural method, it does not necessarily follow that a list of capabilities and functionings can be derived from adherence to such a foundational theory. In other words, what distinguishes procedural from foundational methods is the fact that procedural methods do not derive relevant capabilities and functionings from some ultimate normative value or principle (although such values and principles may play a role in justifying the choice of method) but from an open-ended inquiry into people's actual values.

The first set of procedural methods that we can identify is quantitative analyses. Quantitative analyses uses statistical analysis of how people value certain capabilities, providing insights about which capabilities people find most relevant (Vizard 2010, 1). Ballon (2013, 7; 10–12) argues that we can use statistical data to identify relevant and valuable capabilities in two ways. The first method deduces relevant capabilities and functionings from the values expressed by the surveyed subjects. She calls this *data-driven selection*. Data-driven capability selection merely summarizes the statistical data rather than questioning it. The second method, to the contrary, seeks to confirm the assumptions and hypotheses of economic models against the data sets. Ballon labels these approaches *confirmatory statistical methods*. Confirmatory statistical methods specify hypotheses about human well-being and development and compare these to the statistical data in order to confirm, corroborate, or disprove them.

One major weakness of quantitative analysis, however, is that it does not capture information and data, which cannot be quantified or aggregated (Hodgett and Deneulin 2009, 66–7). Moreover, statistical data is not always available or reliable and is thus not considered. Hodgett and Deneulin (2009, 66) give the example of domestic violence. Although the risk of domestic violence can be considered an important aspect of gender equity, there is often no reliable data available and it is difficult to quantify the experience of domestic violence. Ignoring certain capabilities for pragmatic reasons leaves the outcome of the qualitative analysis incomplete and somewhat random and thus unsuitable for the task of selecting capabilities for human development purposes.

As a consequence, Hodgett and Deneulin (2009, 68) argue, it would be prudent to supplement or replace quantitative analysis with *qualitative analyses*. Qualitative analyses base a list of capabilities on inquiries on the values and preferences of individuals and groups. We can identify two uses of qualitative research within the capability literature: narratives and participatory programs. *Narrative approaches* to the selection of relevant capabilities allow people to make sense of their own experiences and express their needs and values in life stories. Listening to these stories, researchers look for common themes and recurring issues (Hodgett and Deneulin 2009, 74). Whereas statistics aggregate people across race, religion, nationality, ethnicity, and age, narratives place people and their experiences in an environmental, personal, and social context (Hodgett and Deneulin 2009, 70).

Because people's lives and experiences cannot be separated from their environmental and sociocultural setting (Hodgett and Deneulin 2009, 67), it is important to note that there is a risk that their narratives may not reflect real desires, but rather the social norms and cultural values (Biggeri et al. 2006, 68) or the power relations in the group where the selection is made. Thus, Biggeri et al. (2006, 68) argue, the process should be "conductive to the reflective reasoning around individual preferences" in order to (ideally) "detach them from the constraints of the adaption to personal experiences." Consequentially, Biggeri et al. (2006) supplement the narrative approach with a *participatory approach*, which aims at facilitating the critical reflection and discussion among a group of individuals, either with different or similar backgrounds. The participatory method is partly an open approach allowing the participants to exchange ideas and experiences, and partly a critical exercise in which participants reflect on and discuss these ideas and experiences (Chambers 1997, 102).

Generally, the qualitative methods have a number of limitations (Hodgett and Deneulin 2009, 77). First, they are limited in terms of scope (Cooke and Kothari 2001; Frediani 2007, 9). Due to practical constraints, it is often only possible to conduct a small sample of interviews or consultations and thus not necessarily represent the whole population who will be affected by the implementation of a list of capabilities. Second, even if the collection of data were balanced and representative, the researchers may still manipulate the result according to their aims (e.g., by only including the positive or negative responses). Third, people's narratives are influenced by the institutional setting. Not only may the way the interviews or consultations are conducted influence how people express themselves, but people's experiences and languages are also affected by their social and cultural background. It is not always easy to disentangle people's real experiences from these backdrops.

Moreover, a special issue relating to the qualitative methods concerns the *subjectivity* of the people's experiences and the vulnerability to implicit biases and adaptive preferences. Implicit bias is an unconscious attitude someone may have toward other people, groups, or things. Someone may, for example, have a negative view of government intervention and thus oppose tax raises even though he might in the end benefit from such a tax policy. Adaptation of preferences occurs when someone lowers or raises her expectations due to the circumstances she is in. Someone may, for example, find her perspectives so hopeless that she gives up on her dreams, while someone who had something good happen to him may accordingly expect more good things to happen.

It should be noted, however, that some capability scholars have argued that, while some people may suffer from implicit biases and adaptive preferences, people are *in general* aware of their own values and the extent to which they are satisfied (Clark 2009; Barr and Clark 2009) or that evidence of adaptive preferences is inconclusive (Clark and Qizilbash 2008, 536). However, this is not a common view among capability scholars (and moral psychologists). For example, Khader (2009, 2013) identifies several cases where individuals adapt their preferences despite not suffering from any of the traditional ways of thinking about adaptive preferences, such as lack of adequate information, agency, autonomy, or self-interest, while Conradie and Robeyns (2013) and Ibrahim (2011) document that although people's aspirations are less vulnerable to adaptation than the critics may think, they are nevertheless negatively affected by conditions of poverty and oppression.

If this were true, democratic bottom-up approaches to the selection of capabilities risk conflicting with normative standards and principles (Burchardt and Vizard 2011, 99–100). As Nussbaum (2003, 47) argues,

> [s]ome human matters are too important to be left to whim and caprice, or even to the dictates of cultural tradition. To say that education for women, or adequate health care, is not justified just in case some nation believes that it is not justified seems like a capitulation to subjective preferences.

What proponents of procedural methods argue is that creating favorable conditions for preference formation, such as better access to information, more critical reflection, and increased interaction and deliberation, can reduce the risk of preference adaptation. However, all of these measures are *complementary* to the qualitative method and rely on a normative conception of what nonadaptive preferences look like. What is more, it seems that in arguing for the creation of such favorable conditions we already make a judgment about what capabilities and functionings are normatively important, namely those that allow people to form nonadaptive preferences. To wit, qualitative methods cannot constitute a 'pure' procedural approach to selecting capabilities and functionings because it must incorporate some foundational insights in order to avoid the charge of being vulnerable to adaptive preferences and implicit biases.

Can we establish a purely procedural approach to selecting capabilities and functionings? Especially Sen (1999a, 1999, 2001, 2002; Sen and Scanlon 2004; Drèze and Sen 2002) has been a strong proponent of the view that a third procedural method, namely deliberative democracy, can help overcome the issues relating to implicit biases and adaptive preferences.[9] Deliberative democracy, as Anderson (2003, 250) puts it, "is the institutional embodiment of practical reason for a collective agency composed of equal citizens." Through deliberation people are, on the one hand, able to express their values and preferences, while on the other hand, this process forces them to confront the values of themselves and others with good arguments, thus fostering their reasoned revision.

Sen (1999a, chap. 6; 2001, 10–11)[10] argues that deliberative democracy is important for three reasons. First of all, democratic participation is *intrinsically* important because it is a capability in and of itself. Providing access to deliberative democratic procedures thus serves directly as an expansion of people's capability sets. Second, deliberative democracy is *instrumentally* important because it enhances the opportunity for people's opinions to be heard and democratic rights may help to hold policymakers accountable insofar as they have to face people's criticisms and seek their support. Third, and most importantly, deliberative democracy serves a *constructive* role. The constructive role of deliberation is directly aimed at addressing the charge of implicit bias and adaptive preferences.

The formation of *reasoned* values and preferences, Sen (1999a, 153; see also Anderson 2003, 249) argues, crucially depends on public discussion: as people engage in public deliberations, they are forced to confront the biases and adaptive preferences of themselves and others and revise them in light of better evidence.

It seems, then, that a deliberative democratic method can avoid relying on a foundational method because the critical reflection on people's values and preferences is built into the method itself. Even if these critical insights came from normative theory, they would only constitute a contribution to the deliberative exercise.

The deliberative method faces three major issues, however. First, the circumstances surrounding democratic deliberations are often nonideal at best and severely dysfunctional at worst. Consider, for example, that development is often needed in societies with high socioeconomic inequality, low educational levels, and poor access to democratic institutions (such as a free press). Individually, these circumstances may hamper democratic ambitions, but put together they make the prospect of a proper public deliberation extremely weak. Socioeconomic differences have been shown to be reproduced in democratic participation giving more representation (and, presumably, political power) to the better-off (Huber et al. 1997), while a lack of a free press restricts citizens' access to information. Furthermore, as Smith (2014) argues, people are generally bad at deliberating because they suffer from a variety of biases in the process of making decisions. Even well-educated deliberators, Smith argues, fail to be self-critical and give due consideration to the arguments of others. In other words, if these objections hold, the assumptions underlying the constructive role of deliberation are undermined, casting serious doubts on the deliberative democratic method of selecting capabilities.

Second, even if the qualitative and deliberative approaches could solve the issue of biases and adaptive preferences, the deliberative method's requirement of reasoned scrutiny runs contrary to the method's ambition of representing the plural values of deliberators (Argenton and Rossi 2013). For deliberation to lead to the positive construction of shared values and goals, on Sen's deliberative account agents must be "reason giving and autonomous" individuals who are "sufficiently neutral toward competing conceptions of the good" (Argenton and Rossi 2013, 137). Yet, this is quite substantively a liberal understanding of what it means to be a deliberative agent; one in which the deliberators are expected to deliberate in a particular way, namely through reasoned introspection and exchange of reasoned arguments. This is in conflict with Sen's commitment to pluralism, according to Argenton and Rossi, because it only accommodates pluralism in its reasonable forms. By requiring deliberators to scrutinize their own beliefs and values and provide generally acceptable reasons for them, the deliberative method is "an essentially homogenous moralized consensus, based on the unwarranted silencing of some of the most challenging expressions of pluralism" (Argenton and Rossi 2013, 137).[11]

Third, in order to avoid these two objections, as Claassen (2011) and Walzer (1981) point out, deliberative democratic methods must themselves rely on a substantive democratic theory that delineates what a just democratic procedure looks like. For deliberative democracy to constitute a reliable method, we already assume that stakeholders have a range of capabilities and functionings, such as access to robust democratic institutions and information as well as the capacity for critical reflection and deliberation, which in turn requires adequate cognitive skills and access to education (Bohman 1997, 325–6).

Thus, it seems that even on the level of selecting capabilities and functionings, the deliberative method cannot escape the predicament that was outlined at the beginning of this section. Recall that it was here argued that even though procedural methods may adhere to a foundational theory (e.g., deliberative democratic theory) at the level of justifying the method, it does not necessarily follow that we are thereby committed to a list of capabilities and functionings. However, if the practical implementation of a deliberative method indeed requires the capabilities and functionings highlighted by Bohman, it *does* follow that we are committed to a substantive list of capabilities and functionings, namely those that are necessary for a functioning democratic deliberation. Even though the list of capabilities and functionings that follows may be quite minimal and imperfect (Byskov 2017a, 11)—that is, restricted to democratic capabilities and not comprehensive of what is normatively relevant for development—the deliberative democratic method as a purely procedural method is illusive because it does to some extent rely on a foundational method.

In sum, although the procedural methods can address two of the concerns that we identified with the foundational methods—namely lack of democratic legitimacy and contextual sensitivity—selecting capabilities procedurally, either through empirical research or public deliberation, requires that we move beyond a purely procedural method to include insights from a foundational method about what constitutes a just or reliable democratic deliberation. In the final section, two methods, which combine two or more foundational and procedural methods, are explored.

6.5 Mixed (or Multi-stage) Methods

I have in the previous sections identified three general categories of methods for the selection of capabilities and functionings—ad hoc, foundational, and procedural methods—and argued that neither is suitable, on its own, to fulfill the task of selecting capabilities relevant for development purposes: ad hoc methods lack any robust justification of the particular items, 'purely' foundational methods lack democratic and epistemological legitimacy, while 'purely' procedural methods are vulnerable to subjectivism.

The silver lining, however, is that both the foundational and procedural methods may satisfy *different aspects* of a list of capabilities. On the one hand, democratic and participative exercises are important because they capture the *process* aspect of a selection of capabilities (Sen 1997; Robeyns 2003, 69). In short, it makes a difference in terms of legitimacy whether a list of capabilities is derived from normative theory or has been through a democratic process, even if the lists are identical (Jaggar 2006; Robeyns 2005). Moreover, local stakeholders may provide information about the local socioeconomic conditions and social norms that development experts and policy-makers have little access to (Byskov 2017b). On the other hand, however, democratic bottom-up approaches may reproduce unjust sociocultural norms and local power relations (Claassen 2011, 496; Nussbaum 2003, 47). Setting out normative standards and principles is thus an important aspect of a justifiable list of capabilities that can only be fulfilled by a theoretical exercise (Claassen 2011, 498–9; Byskov 2017a, 4–5).

Some capability scholars have attempted to capture this duality of aspects by adopting or proposing *mixed (or multi-stage) methods* for the selection of capabilities and functionings. Mixed or multi-stage methods combine two or more foundational and procedural methods in order to create an integrated approach to the selection of capabilities and functioning. Robeyns (2003, 71), for example, argues that a list of capabilities

> should be drawn up in at least two stages. The first stage can involve drawing up a kind of "ideal" list, unconstrained by limitations of data or measurement design, or of socioeconomic or political feasibility. The second stage would be drawing up a more pragmatic list which takes such constraints into account.

By integrating procedural and foundational aspects, in this way, the ambition is to capture what Sen (1997) has labeled the *comprehensive outcome* of selecting capabilities. As Sen argues, we should distinguish between the culmination outcome and the comprehensive outcome of a list of capabilities. While the culmination outcome only takes into consideration whether the final list of capabilities can be justified—that is, none of the items on the list violates principles of justice—the comprehensive outcome also considers the justifiability of the procedure by which the list was brought about. Mixed (or multi-stage) methods aim to justify both the procedure as well as the particular list of capabilities.

Robeyns herself does not specify her mixed (or multi-stage) method further, nor does she take a stance on the normative relationship between the two or more stages. Within the capability literature we can identify two specific kinds of mixed (or multi-stage) methods. *Comparative methods* start out by identifying an abstract and idealized list of capabilities in theory, which is then specified through an empirical or deliberative exercise. It is important to note that in cases of conflict, top-down comparative methods hold that the list derived from theory has overriding status. (As such, the empirical/deliberative exercise is merely for comparative purposes, making the method decidedly top-down.) *Synthesizing methods*, to the contrary, embraces the potential conflict between lists derived from, respectively, theory and empirical/deliberative exercises by facilitating a dialectical 'conversation' between the two stages. This conversation can have two purposes: on the one hand, the empirical/deliberative exercise can inform the (normative) theory while, on the other hand, the (normative) theory can provide a critical view on the empirically or deliberatively developed list. In the following, I discuss both methods in turn and argue that the task of selecting capabilities for human development purposes is best managed by adopting a synthesizing method.

Brock (2009), Burchardt and Vizard (2011), and Holland (2014) adopt a 'two-stage' method, which informs and specifies an abstract normative theory through empirical or deliberative means. While Holland (2014, 188–92) follows Nussbaum in specifying ten central capabilities and showing how they are affected by local environmental conditions, Burchardt and Vizard (2011, 92) combine " 'bottom-up' deliberative/participative strategies on the one hand, and internationally recognized human rights standards on the other." Brock (2009, 5) similarly argues that real discussions on public policy "can usefully inform" her cosmopolitan account of global justice.

The first stage of the selection process aims at identifying overlapping and shared ideal principles—for example, in the international human rights treaties and conventions (Burchardt and Vizard 2011, 100–2), in a hypothetical overlapping consensus (Holland 2014, 188–92), or in a cosmopolitan account of global justice based on an original position approach (Brock 2009, chap. 3)—which can provide a normative basis for the list of capabilities. The second stage plays either or both of two primary roles within top-down comparative methods. On the one hand, it may adapt or refine the abstract list to local socioeconomic and environmental circumstances, taking such constraints into concern (Burchardt and Vizard 2011, 102–3; Robeyns 2003, 70–1). Brock (2009, part II), for example, investigates five discussions within public policy, which she uses to inform and refine her theory of global justice (Brock 2009, part III). As such it satisfies the epistemological objection that theorists may not know what matters to the local stakeholders.

On the other hand, the second stage may also satisfy the issue of democratic legitimacy by including "a process of deliberation and debate, giving the general public and those at risk of discrimination and disadvantage a defining role in identifying and justifying the selection of central and basic capabilities" (Burchardt and Vizard 2011, 102).

The main issue with such two-stage methods as the ones adopted by Brock (2009), Burchardt and Vizard (2011), and Holland (2014) is that the two stages may arrive at conflicting lists of capabilities. That is, there may be cases where the second empirical/deliberative stage identifies capabilities, which do not only supplement the normative theory's list of capabilities, but are actually incompatible with it. How should such conflicts be resolved? Brock (2009, 73–4), Burchardt and Vizard (2011, 104) and Holland (2014, 137–8) all stress the priority of the list of capabilities derived from normative theory over the list of capabilities derived from an empirical or deliberative exercise. In this sense, the method ultimately becomes top-down, imposing the normative theory on the people to whom it applies, while the empirical/deliberative exercise merely poses as a comparison and confirmation of the normative list.

If this is true, then the top-down comparative method cannot meet standards of democratic legitimacy: while it is true that granting overriding priority to the list derived from normative theory ensures that the list of capabilities arrived at in the second stage does not violate basic normative principles—including a list of basic capabilities—in practice it has the consequence that a list of capabilities only has validity *insofar as it aligns with* the normative theory and its (substantive) list of capabilities. In other words, the empirical/deliberative process cannot in itself (or only secondarily—if at all) justify a certain selection of capabilities. But this ability is arguably the hallmark of a comprehensive outcome. A selection of capabilities gains democratic legitimacy exactly because it is not imposed on the people to whom it applies. This should lead us to reject the top-down comparative method as suitable for the selection of capabilities and functionings for development purposes.

How can we retain democratic legitimacy while minimizing the risk that the final list of capabilities violates basic normative principles (assuming that there will always be some tension between the two)? A second set of mixed methods may promise to rectify this democratic shortcoming. *Synthesizing methods* to the selection of capabilities accord equal priority to the two (or more) stages and engage them in an ongoing dialectical dialogue with the aim of enhancing and improving both the normative theory and the democratic decision-making process. Rather than being antagonistic, then, the two (or more) stages are seen as different contributions that provide critical insights to the process of making a selection of capabilities that is, on the one hand, normatively justifiable and, on the other hand, democratically and contextually sensitive. In the following I shortly discuss three such synthesizing methods to the selection of capabilities.

Alkire (2002), Claassen (2011), and Khader (2011) all adopt (or propose to adopt) a three-stage method, which engages in a dialectical or dialogical exercise between theoretical reflection, empirical investigation, and public deliberation. The three stages are, respectively, (1) from practice to theory, (2) from (refined) theory to practice, and (3) a synthesis. The dialectical dialogue is present at all stages of Alkire's, Claassen's, and Khader's methods. On the first stage, Alkire, Claassen, and Khader start out by identifying a normative theory, which can and should be supplemented or refined through a participatory (Alkire 2002, 43–7), empirical (Claassen 2011, 504–5), or deliberative (Khader 2011, 20–1) exercise. The reasons they provide for this are different, however.

Alkire (2002, 43–4), for example, identifies a preliminary list of basic capabilities, which she then uses to facilitate a process of practical reasoning with her participants in order to further specify the list of capabilities to local values and circumstances. To Claassen (2011, 504), the empirical investigation is meant to address the objection from epistemology: the theorist cannot by herself know what is relevant to those who are affected by a list of capabilities and she must therefore "learn from public debates about capabilities [or] even conduct social scientific research to find out which capabilities people value most" and with suitable modification allow the results of this practical investigation to influence and enhance her ideal list of capabilities. As Claassen (2011, 505) further puts it, "[t]he philosopher's individual epistemological limits are compensated for by drawing upon the knowledge of (many) others." Khader (2011, 21), on her part, aims to address the objection from democratic legitimacy, arguing that "we want people to be judged by a conception of flourishing that is widely perceived as legitimate."

In the second stage, this refined normative theory is then used as a starting point for a process of practical reasoning (Alkire 2002, 46), or offered for public deliberation and endorsement (Claassen 2011, 501) or as an input in a participatory dialogue with local stakeholders (Khader 2011, 22). Thus, where the first stage worked from practice to theory, the second stage of their methods moves from (refined) theory back to practice. Again, the reasons Alkire, Claassen, and Khader give for this move are different. The primary reason for offering the refined normative theory for public deliberation and endorsement is primarily a matter of democratic legitimacy, according to Claassen (2011, 500–2). Claassen (2011, 501) admits that if a list were to be applied directly and solely based on authority of the theorist, it would indeed lack democratic legitimacy. Yet, as Claassen (2011, 501) further argues, the theorist should not demand compliance with her list independently of public deliberation but rather offer it "as an input into a democratic process run by others."

To Khader, meanwhile, the second stage of her method has epistemological motivation. Whereas the first stage of her method intends to specify a normative theory—in particular, a cross-cultural conception of human flourishing based on a deliberative exercise—in the second stage this refined normative theory (i.e., of human flourishing) can help identify an unjust state of affairs (in Khader's (2011, 22) case, whether someone is suffering from adaptive preferences). Similarly, Alkire intends the second stage to have epistemic consequences for her participants: by engaging them and challenging their beliefs and values, Alkire (2002, 46) aims to make her participants reflect on, reason about, and refine the list of capabilities and functionings they find valuable and the reasons why they do so based on their own personal, historical, and socioeconomic context.

The third stage of Alkire's, Claassen's, and Khader's methods serves as a synthesis where normative and descriptive content form a critical input that aims to enable local stakeholders—participants in development projects (Alkire); deliberators (Claassen); individuals suffering from adaptive preferences (Khader)—to make informed decisions about which capabilities are normatively relevant, for themselves or in general. As Claassen (2011, 505) argues, "the fact that a group of people empirically holds the belief that realizing capability *x* is a moral demand does not mean that these beliefs are morally correct."

Hence, Alkire (2002, 46), Claassen (2011, 505), and Khader (2011, 22) hold that we need to engage in a critical dialogue with stakeholders. Through this critical dialogue the democratic and epistemological concerns come together. On the one hand, whereas Burchardt and Vizard (2011) and Holland's (2014) mixed approaches endorses paternalistic intervention when encountered with a potential source of reproduction of an unjust state of affairs, Alkire's, Claassen's, and Khader's methods hold that the decision ultimately lies with the public itself.[12] On the other hand, whereas Burchardt and Vizard's (2011) and Holland's (2014) approaches only sought to confirm the normative theory through an empirical exercise, Alkire, Claassen, and Khader hold that it is the normative theory that must inform the individual or public deliberation process.

It might be argued, however, that the synthesizing method does not avoid the problem of indeterminacy that the comparative method resolves by giving overriding normative status to normative theory. That is, because the synthesizing method gives equal status or priority to the foundationally and procedurally established lists of capabilities, it cannot resolve disputes that arise between these lists. We can respond to this criticism in two ways. First, disagreements are an inherent part of political discourse. Within political discourse we often have to make compromises that result in nonideal solutions. That does not mean that these solutions are unjust. Nor does it, second, mean that we should discontinue process of deliberation of coming to a mutual understanding. What we disagree on now may be resolved in the future. Thus, what the synthesizing method proposes is an ongoing process that may provide a nonideal list of capabilities and functionings, which is under continued scrutiny and revision as we repeat the stages of dialectic deliberation described earlier.

In sum, a synthesizing method as a method for the selection of capabilities has the most potential, I contend, as a method for selecting capabilities for development purposes. This is so because it manages to address several of the concerns that we have raised against other methods, most importantly normative justifiability, democratic legitimacy, and contextual sensitivity.

6.6 Synthesizing Methods, Local Authority, and Mediating Experts

In the previous section, I analyzed and discussed the three-stage synthesizing method for the selection of normatively relevant capabilities and functionings. A synthesizing method integrates both foundational and procedural methods in a critical discussion and synthesis about what is normatively relevant for a development agenda. Throughout this book, I have made several claims, however, and in this final section I will inquire whether—and positively conclude that—the synthesizing method, as I have defined and specified it, is compatible with these claims. I first investigate the synergies between the claim to local authority before I argue that the synthesizing method is vulnerable to miscommunications, such as the ones identified in Chapter 4, and that we need to employ mediating experts when applying the method in practice.

6.6.1 Synthesizing Methods and Local Authority

The first question that we need to ask is, how does the synthesizing method square with the arguments for more local authority that I expanded on in Chapters 3 and 4? Does the synthesizing method respect the criteria for nondomination? Can it accommodate the two domains of authority—political and expert?

Recall that in Chapter 3 I defined the claim to local authority minimally as the claim that local stakeholders should be granted more authority in matters of their own development (including in the setting of a development agenda). This is so in two regards. On the one hand, it is a claim to grant local stakeholders more political authority. In Chapter 3, I grounded this claim in a republican theory, which holds that the political process of setting and adopting a development agenda must respect certain procedural constraints so as not to be imposed on the local stakeholders on an arbitrary basis. On the other hand, the claim to local authority may also be interpreted as the claim that local stakeholders should be granted more expert authority in the socioscientific decision-making process. In Chapter 4, I argued that local stakeholders who possess contributory expertise—relevant tacit or embodied knowledge—should be granted expert authority.

The synergies between the synthesizing method and the claim to local authority are at least threefold. First, the synthesizing method certainly grants local stakeholders political decision-making rights. Contrary to the other multi-stage method, comparative methods, the synthesizing method does not contain a clause that can overrule the popular voice. By engaging critically with local stakeholders, the method respects them as moral and political agents that are capable of and have the right to decide on matters of their own development. In order to consolidate this right to political authority, moreover, it is straightforward to imagine that the synthesizing method can incorporate the kinds of initiatives needed to counter the risk of public and private domination that I discussed in Chapter 3.

Second, the multiple stages of the synthesizing method embody the distinction between the political and the expert domains of authority. Within the method, the domain of expertise—which I discussed in Chapter 4—is represented by the idea that a holistic and comprehensive procedure needs to incorporate critical insights. Such critical insights come from development experts, which, I argued, should include local stakeholders with relevant tacit or embodied knowledge. Conversely, a comprehensive method, as I have insisted throughout, must be democratically legitimate. This commitment to democratic legitimacy is represented within the synthesizing method by the inclusion of procedural methods through which all (local) stakeholders have the political authority to have their voice heard. By integrating normative insights derived from foundational methods with the democratic sensitivity of the procedural methods, the synthesizing method is dialectic and holistic in the sense indicated by the distinction between two domains.

Third, it is important to note that I have not advocated an interpretation of the claim to local authority that would entail a full transfer of authority to local stakeholders. Rather, in Chapters 3 and 4 I argued that in regard to both political and expert authority, the claim to local authority should be interpreted so as to leave room for external intervention (within the limits of republican theory). The synthesizing method likewise leaves room for external involvement in the setting of a development agenda by holding that a selection of normatively relevant capabilities and functionings must be decided through a critical deliberative process involving both nonlocal stakeholders and local stakeholders.

In sum, the synergies between the claim to local authority, as I defined and specified it in Chapters 3 and 4, and the synthesizing method support my argument that selecting normatively relevant capabilities and functionings for a development agenda is best managed through a mixed (or multi-stage) method—in particular the method that I have labeled the synthesizing method. That is not to say, however, that the synthesizing method does not suffer from certain problems when applied in practice. In the following, I argue that the synthesizing method is vulnerable to the kinds of miscommunications that I identified in Chapter 4.

6.6.2 Synthesizing Methods and Mediating Experts

In this section, I show how the integration of two (or more) stages is vulnerable to miscommunications, such as the ones identified in Chapter 4.

Recall that miscommunications arise between two (or more) different stakeholders due to a lack of interactional expertise on behalf of one or both of the stakeholders. Interactional expertise is the ability to communicate properly and efficiently in relation to the knowledge of other stakeholders. A lack of interactional expertise, I argued, manifests itself in terms of the epistemological and ontological assumptions the different parties employ, in terms of power, as well as practical disagreements (Brand and Karvonen 2007, 22–4). In the following, I argue that the synthesizing method is vulnerable to the issue of miscommunication, and consequently that we need to employ mediating experts when applying the method in practice.

The synthesizing method seems to satisfy three important criteria of a development agenda, namely contextual sensitivity, normative justification, and democratic legitimacy. However, Alkire's, Claassen's, and Khader's versions of the synthesizing method are all vulnerable to miscommunications insofar as they attempt to incorporate theoretical insights into a democratic decision-making procedure. Even if the normative and descriptive theory, which is offered as an input to the democratic procedure, has been refined through an empirical or deliberative exercise, it is quite plausible that it is still quite different from the preferences that the local stakeholders may hold—for example due to adaptive preferences (Khader) or their "ideological commitments, considerations of personal status, power relations, electoral strategies, etc." (Claassen 2011, 504)—and hence it is necessary to engage local stakeholders in a critical dialogue in the first place. In addition to high levels of socioeconomic inequalities, low educational levels, and poor access to democratic institutions, implicit and deliberative biases (Smith 2014) may hamper any prospect of the third democratic stage yielding a fruitful result. As such, the synthesizing method will necessarily involve a large variety of different stakeholders and experts who may come from different professional, sociocultural, and epistemological backgrounds. As I documented in Chapter 4, such differences are likely to cause breakdowns in communication in a variety of ways.

The final stage of the synthesizing method is thus vulnerable to the issue of miscommunication when applied in practice. How can we expect that local stakeholders should be receptive to the kind of critical insights that Claassen and Khader envision? While Claassen merely leaves the decision-making process to deliberators (with the normative philosopher providing external criticism), Alkire and Khader come closer to expressing what I shall suggest in the following by arguing that we need to engage in a dialogue between development experts and local stakeholders.

My argument is that for the synthesizing method to be successful and fruitful when applied in practice, it should be supplemented by certain forms of mediating expertise, such as the five types I identified in Chapter 4. In the first stage of a synthesizing method, enriching the theory through empirical means, the interdisciplinary expert, the meta-expert, and the civic expert could prove to be especially valuable. While the meta-expert makes judgments about who should make contributions to the theory, the interdisciplinary expert works across disciplines and investigates where insights from one pool of knowledge can contribute to creating solutions within another discipline (Brand and Karvonen 2007, 26–8). The interdisciplinary expert may, at this stage of the method, for example, draw on sociological and anthropological insights to improve an economic analysis or a theory of justice. The civic expert can engage with the public in order to incorporate their experiential knowledge.

In the second stage of a synthesizing method, which works from theory to practice, the outreach expert and the civic expert will be especially valuable in making the theory intelligible to the local stakeholders and expanding their informational basis when engaging in a deliberative exercise. Recall that the aim of the outreach expert, according to Brand and Karvonen (2007, 26), is to communicate and disseminate scientific knowledge to the public and thereby increase their level of knowledge and information, while the civic expert engages with the public in a critical dialogue on these issues. The outreach and civic experts may be able to translate the normative and descriptive theory into a language that is intelligible to the local stakeholders and make clear exactly how it impacts their daily lives.

Finally, the civic expert may, together with the political expert (and possibly also the outreach expert), be especially important for the success of a synthesizing method in setting a development agenda. The civic expert (and the outreach expert) can engage the local stakeholders in a critical dialogue and deliberation with the aim of identifying and highlighting common concerns and points of agreement and exchanging viewpoints and reasons. Meanwhile, the political expert, adept at negotiating politically between various stakeholders, will be instrumental in helping the participants in the democratic process synthesize the (refined) theoretical input and the concerns raised in the deliberative exercise into a widely endorsed development agenda.

In sum, all three stages of a synthesizing method can benefit from the involvement of various types of mediating experts. The five types of mediating experts I identified in Chapter 4 can enable local stakeholders, with the input from external experts, to arrive at a reasoned and widely endorsed development agenda. Making these connections, I propose, makes the synthesizing method practically plausible as a method for the selection of capabilities and functionings for a development agenda.

6.7 Concluding Remarks

In sum, Chapters 5 and 6 have answered the third and final question that I set out at the beginning of this book: by which method should we select normatively relevant capabilities for a development agenda? In Chapter 5, I set out four criteria concerning how we should evaluate these methods, and in this chapter I identified, analyzed, and discussed four general categories of methods for the selection of normatively relevant capabilities and functionings, comprising fifteen more specific methods. *Ad hoc methods* base a list of capabilities on the values of the researcher or practical concerns; *foundational methods* derive a list from technical knowledge and reasoning; *procedural methods* identify capabilities through either empirical studies or a deliberative process; and *mixed (or multi-stage) methods* integrate two or more foundational and procedural methods.

I have argued that the first three methodologies mentioned earlier—ad hoc, technocratic, and procedural methods—have serious shortcomings when applied to the task of setting a development agenda. Generally, these shortcomings are either a lack of contextual sensitivity, normative justification, or democratic legitimacy. However, I argued that these shortcomings can be ameliorated by adopting a mixed (or multi-stage) method.

In particular, I have argued that we would do best to adopt the method that I have labeled *synthesizing methods*. Synthesizing methods aim to engage critically with local stakeholders in a three-stage procedure. While the purpose of the first stage is to enrich the normative and descriptive theory through empirical and deliberative exercises, the second stage offers this refined theory as an input to a democratic procedure with the aim of enhancing the informational bases of the participants. Lastly, in the third stage, local stakeholders engage in a critical deliberation with the ideal outcome of an informed and widely endorsed list of capabilities and functionings. Synthesizing methods, I argued, can satisfy our concerns about contextual sensitivity, normative justification, and democratic legitimacy.

Finally, I argued that the synthesizing method is synergetic and complementary to the claim to local authority, as I defined and specified it in Chapters 3 and 4, but it needs to be supplemented by the five types of experts that I identified in Chapter 4 in order to be practically useful for setting a development agenda. The interdisciplinary expert, the meta-expert, and the civic expert are especially valuable in the first stage of the method, when the technocratic theory is enriched by the local stakeholders' experiential knowledge and concerns. The second stage will especially involve the outreach expert and the civic expert, who can disseminate, illuminate, and clarify the refined theory for the local stakeholders, ideally presenting it in a way that makes it relevant to them and their lives. The civic expert and the political expert play the largest roles in the third, synthesizing stage, which engages local stakeholders in a critical deliberative exercise with the aim of crystalizing the discussion into a widely endorsed development agenda.

Notes

1 An overview of the general and specific methods, identified within the capability literature, and their main proponents can be found in Table 6.1.
2 It should be noted, however, that Alkire (2002) undertook a similar endeavor in regard to the different list of capabilities and functionings in the capability literature. Alkire, however, did not engage in the critical analysis and discussion of *how* these lists were brought about – a gap that this chapter will fill.
3 See also Alkire (2008) for a similar conclusion.
4 It should be noted that each of these terms might carry different connotations depending on one's discipline. I shall here use the terms in the philosophical tradition and otherwise explain exactly how they are to be understood.
5 Each specific method may be more suitable for other tasks, such as the development of a capability theory of justice, particular empirical studies, or the conceptualization of a specific domain, such as education or health care.
6 It should be noted, however, that Nussbaum (2000, 83) acknowledges that her list of capabilities does not include all characteristics that we recognize as human (such as the propensity for violence and cruelty), but only those capabilities that can be morally defended.
7 See also Alkire (2002, 36–43) for three additional issues that make Nussbaum's overlapping consensus method unsuitable for development purposes.
8 As Vizard (2007, 237) argues, such lists are not fixed or set in stone, but rather under continuous revision.
9 Especially Crocker (2008, 2005), Drydyk (2005), and Anderson (1999, 2003) have been at the forefront of conceptualizing a capability theory of deliberative democracy.
10 See also Crocker (2008, chap. 9) for an in-depth discussion of the importance of democracy, especially in relation to the way it enhances people's agency.
11 Consider, for example, as Argenton and Rossi (2013, 137) do, a religious person who believes that questioning her own beliefs would condemn her to Dante's Seventh Circle of Hell reserved for blasphemers.
12 See, however, Claassen (2014), who does allow for some paternalist interventions to ensure basic agential functionings.

7 An Inclusive Framework for Setting Development Agendas

In this book, I have developed what I call an inclusive framework for setting development agendas. This inclusive framework aims to integrate different sources of knowledge, such as philosophical theory, empirical analyses, deliberative exercises, and not least, the tacit and experiential knowledge of local stakeholders. In this concluding chapter, I provide a final overview of the argument that I have given in this book and sum up some of my conclusions. While the framework that I propose in this book has a quite specific focus, I shall here take the opportunity to look forward and speculate on how my framework can be applied not only to future development agendas—including the monitoring and evaluation of progress—but also to other development tasks, such as the design of specific development projects.

I begin by restating the three initial questions—what kinds of goals?, who should participate?, and how?—that motivated the inquiries of this book (section 7.1). In section 7.2, I provide a summary of my argument, including an overview of my proposed framework for the setting of a development agenda, while section 7.3 spells out how the book contributes to the literature. Finally, I consider how my framework can contribute to discussions outside of the particular context of a development agenda (section 7.4).

7.1 Three Fundamental Questions Revisited

What is a development agenda? A development agenda, as I have defined it, is a normative convention, agreement, decree, or aspiration that specifies a set of goals that should be achieved by international, national, and local development efforts, such as concrete development interventions and projects, as well as national public policies. As such, the goals that are included on a development agenda have the potential to have a real impact on the socioeconomic structure and appearance of the world. It is thus important that we are able to select the goals of a development agenda in a way that can be defended and justified.

I opened this book by arguing that before we can even begin to identify specific development goals, we need to take a step back and consider three fundamental questions. In addressing these fundamental questions, we can provide a justification of our development agenda. The three questions are as follows: what *kinds* of development goals should a development agenda include, *who* should be involved in setting the development agenda, and by which *method* should they go about selecting particular development goals? How we answer these questions might crucially influence what goals we find normatively relevant for a development agenda.

First of all, I argued that there are different kinds of development goals. A development agenda may concentrate on goals that address people's basic needs, such as food, water, and shelter. It may concern economic goals or it may only include those goals that are immediately achievable. It may focus on distinguishing those goals that give us the most utility for our investment. Whatever the focus of our development agenda, it will influence the particular goals that it includes. Thus the first question that we need to ask when setting a development agenda is *what kinds of goals should a development agenda include?*

Second, several stakeholders may claim to have an interest in specifying what goals development should achieve. While donor countries have an interest in seeing their money well spent, local stakeholders will want the aid to address their needs. Development experts also hold their particular views on what good development is. Although all of these stakeholders might agree on how a development agenda should look, this is not necessarily so. Thus the second question we should ask is *who has a legitimate claim to authority in the process of setting a development agenda?*

Third, we can employ many different methods for the selection of normatively relevant development goals. We may derive goals from a normative theory, such as a theory of justice or human rights theory, or we may want our agenda to be more empirically founded on qualitative or quantitative analyses. We may want our development agenda to reflect the values of local stakeholders and their societies, or we may engage them in a critical deliberation with the aim of challenging unjust social norms. The third fundamental question that we need to ask when setting a development agenda therefore concerns *by which method should we select normatively relevant development goals?*

In this book, I have argued that we can address these three fundamental questions by adopting an integrated and inclusive framework that aims to engage local stakeholders in a critical deliberation about which capabilities and functionings should be included on a development agenda. In the next section, I elaborate on this framework and how it addresses the three fundamental questions.

7.2 An Inclusive Framework for Setting Development Agendas

What has been argued in this book? At which conclusions have I arrived? In this book, I have argued that we should adopt an inclusive framework when selecting normatively relevant goals for a development agenda. The framework that I have proposed in this book has the following three general characteristics:

- First, the goals of a development agenda are best conceptualized in terms of capabilities and functionings. Capabilities are the real freedom that people have to do or be certain things; functionings are capabilities that have been realized.
- Second, local stakeholders should be granted both political and expert authority in the setting of a development agenda. Politically, the claim to local authority is best accounted for with reference to republican theory, which safeguards local stakeholders against arbitrary domination, while expert authority is best granted to local stakeholders on the basis of their tacit or embodied knowledge about local socioeconomic and environmental conditions.
- Third, the best method for setting a development agenda is to follow a multi-stage process that aims to foster critical engagement between different stakeholders, such as local agents, government policymakers, and external development experts. In order to facilitate this critical engagement, the process should be guided by a variety of mediating experts.

In Chapter 2, I argued that a development agenda should be conceptualized in terms of capabilities and functionings. *Capabilities* are the real freedom to do or be certain things—that is, the activities that we are able to undertake ('doings') and the kinds of persons we are able to be ('beings'). Having the *real freedom* to do or be certain things means that one has all the required means necessary to achieve that doing and being if one wishes to. That is, it is not merely the formal freedom to do or be something, but the substantial opportunity to achieve it. Someone might, for example, have the formal freedom to vote at the elections in the sense that she has a right to do so and that no one will stop her from doing so, but she might lack the substantial possibility to vote because the closest voting station is 200 kilometers away and she does not own a car and does not have the physical ability to walk such a distance. Conversely, someone may be living close to the voting station but still does not have the real freedom to vote because females are not permitted to vote in that particular society. Capabilities are thus real freedoms in the sense that they are corrected for any potential impediments. *Functionings* simply denote those capabilities that have been achieved, whether voluntarily or by chance.

As such, the concept of capabilities and functionings addresses the first question concerning the kinds of goals that a development agenda should include. A focus on capabilities and functionings, I have argued, has advantages over other kinds of development goals because it changes the focus from means (the resources people have) to ends (what they are able to do and be with those resources and goods). This shift in focus is justified because resources and goods alone do not ensure that people are free to or have the possibility to utilize them. That is, what people are actually able to do or be with a certain set of means is contingent upon the particular individual and socioeconomic and environmental circumstances. Conceptualizing development goals in terms of capabilities and functionings captures this aspect of human development: a development agenda on this view should accommodate the diversity of human life by acknowledging the factors that influence what people can or cannot do or be.

In Chapter 3, I argued that while aid donors and development experts have traditionally been in charge of setting the development agenda (in particular, the Millennium Development Goals), development scholars have in the past two decades argued that local stakeholders should have a greater say in this process. I have labeled this *the claim to local authority*. The claim to local authority can be interpreted as a claim for local stakeholders to have more *political authority* and/or *expert authority*. A claim to political authority is the claim that local stakeholders have the right to be involved in and influence the political decision-making process because of the impact that a development agenda will have on their lives. The claim to expert authority is the claim that local stakeholders have expert knowledge, which is relevant and valuable for the setting of a development agenda, and thus cannot be ignored.

I further defended the claim to local political authority by specifying it with the help of republican theory. Republicanism is the idea that people should enjoy *political freedom*, understood as the *absence of domination*. A person or a group is subject to domination—that is, lacks political freedom—insofar as another person or group has the power to arbitrarily interfere with the choices and actions of that person or group, whether or not that power is invoked (Pettit 1999, 165). As such, the claim has not been that local stakeholders are the only political authority. Rather, granting local stakeholders political authority in this sense means that they should be included in the decision-making process and be respected by both lawmakers and law-enforcers.

In Chapter 4, I argued that local stakeholders should likewise be granted more expert authority. I did so by introducing what I call 'third wave development expertise.' Third wave expertise builds on first and second wave conceptions of expertise: while the first wave grants expert authority merely to traditional experts and scientists, the second wave extends expertise to include laypeople. The idea behind second wave expertise is, on the one hand, that the traditional sciences function much in the same way as ordinary social relations and, on the other hand, that laypeople have knowledge that is scientifically significant. Third wave development expertise, meanwhile, provides a normative view of expertise, which, although extending expertise beyond the traditional development experts, aims to delimit what counts as legitimate expert knowledge. Thus, again, the claim has not been that local stakeholders are the only authoritative experts in matters of their own development but rather that they hold legitimate knowledge that is significant for the setting of a development agenda.

Thus, Chapters 3 and 4 addressed the second fundamental question concerning who should be involved in the setting of a development agenda. In both chapters, I carved out a significant space for local stakeholder involvement and authority in setting a development agenda while retaining the necessity of involving other authorities, most importantly development experts, in this task.

In Chapters 5 and 6, I finally turned to investigate by which method(ology) we should identify normatively relevant goals for a development agenda. While several methods have been proposed within the human development and capability literature, I argued that we first need to identify by which *criteria* these methods should be evaluated. Accordingly, in Chapter 5, I argued that a suitable method for the selection of capabilities and functionings for a development agenda should satisfy four general criteria.

First, the criterion of methodological justification holds that it is necessary to make the methodology used explicit and scrutinize it according to the standards of the relevant methodological discipline(s). Second, the criterion of normative justification demands that the method and its list of capabilities and functionings can be at least minimally justified according to normative standards. Based on my defense of the claim to local authority, the criterion of democratic legitimacy, third, states that a suitable method for the selection of capabilities should be able to represent the values and preferences of the people to whom the list of capabilities applies by including them in the socioscientific and political decision-making process. Finally, the criterion of contextual sensitivity holds that a suitable method must be able to adapt to the context and adjust its scope according to whether the selection of capabilities is being applied at a global, regional, national, or local level.

In Chapter 6, I identified fifteen proposed methods for the selection of capabilities and functionings and categorized them within four general methodologies: ad hoc, foundational, procedural, and mixed (or multi-stage) methods. Ad hoc methods, I argued, base their selection of capabilities on ad hoc considerations; foundational methods on an ultimate normative value or principle; and procedural methods on more open-ended, democratic information; while mixed (or multi-stage) methods employ technocratic and procedural methods in conjunction.

Based on the four criteria specified in the previous chapter, I argued that selecting capabilities and functionings for a development agenda is best managed by adopting a mixed (or multi-stage) method. Ad hoc methods were dismissed because of their lack of methodological and normative justification, and foundational methods were also dismissed due to a lack of democratic legitimacy and contextual sensitivity, while procedural methods were found vulnerable to implicit biases and adaptive preferences and hence were found to be a violation of the criterion of normative justification. Consequently, I argued that mixed (or multi-stage) methods—in particular the set of methods that I labeled *synthesizing methods*—could provide both methodological and normative justifications, and could satisfy the criteria of democratic legitimacy and contextual sensitivity.

Synthesizing methods adopt a three-stage method, which engages in a dialectical or dialogical exercise between theoretical reflection, empirical investigation, and public deliberation. The three stages are (1) from practice to theory, (2) from (refined) theory to practice, and (3) a synthesis. In the first stage, a normative, foundational theory is supplemented or refined through a procedural exercise, which in the second stage is then offered for public deliberation and endorsement or as an input into a participatory dialogue with local stakeholders. Finally, the third stage of the critical theory method serves as a synthesis, where normative and descriptive content form a critical input that aims to enable local stakeholders to make informed decisions about which capabilities and functionings are normatively relevant, to themselves or in general.

Synthesizing methods have the most potential, I argued, as a method for setting a development agenda. This is so because they manage to address several of the concerns that we have raised against other methods, most importantly normative justifiability, democratic legitimacy, and contextual sensitivity.

7.3 Contributions of the Book

What are the novel contributions of this book? How does it add to the existing literature on (human) development, the capability approach, democracy in development, and the selection of development goals? I believe that the book offers numerous novel discussions and concepts to the literature. In this section, I briefly consider what these contributions of the book are. While some of these contributions can be found in individual chapters, others only follow from reading the book as an entity. I begin by highlighting three contributions of the book as a whole and the framework that it presents, before I turn to emphasize some of the more particular additions to the literature of the individual chapters.

First of all, the book offers the first systematic approach to setting development agendas. In Chapter 1, I argued that we need to take a step back and consider three fundamental questions when setting a development agenda, namely how to conceptualize development goals, who to include in the process, and how to select relevant goals. This systematic approach, I contend, provides a blueprint for future efforts to set out development agendas at local, international, and global levels.

The second way in which the book contributes to the literature is by developing an inclusive framework for the setting of development agendas. This framework aims to integrate different sources of knowledge when deciding on what goals to set out for development. The idea of third wave development expertise, presented in Chapter 4, and the synthesizing method for selecting capabilities, defended in Chapter 6, provide practically oriented concepts to put this inclusive framework into practice by encouraging and mediating the exchange of knowledge between relevant stakeholders, such as academic researchers, development scholars, NGOs, politicians, and not least, local populations.

The third contribution of the book consists in the philosophical defense throughout of the rights of local stakeholders to be included in discussions on their own development. While this is not the first defense of a more democratic approach to development, in Chapter 3 I find a normative grounding for this defense in republican theory. Proponents of stakeholder rights and democratic development, I argue, have good reasons to adopt the concepts and arguments of republican theory.

Fourth, in Chapter 4 I developed a novel conceptualization of development expertise, which I labeled third wave development expertise.

A fifth contribution of the book lies in the argument that the identification of normatively relevant capabilities and functionings for a development agenda needs to be facilitated by someone who can mediate between the different stakeholders. Recall that in Chapter 4 I argued that the relationship between different stakeholders is vulnerable to miscommunications insofar as all or some of the parties lack *interactional expertise*, the ability to communicate meaningfully with other participants. While development experts may lack interactional expertise insofar as they are unable to make their findings intelligible to local stakeholders, local stakeholders may likewise be unable to communicate their experiential knowledge in a way that can be understood by the experts. Because, as I argued in Chapter 6, we need to engage in a critical dialogue between different stakeholders, this process is vulnerable to miscommunications in the sense described above. Consequently, I have argued that we need to mediate this process. In Chapter 4, I identified five types of mediating experts that could facilitate this process: the outreach expert, the interdisciplinary expert, the meta-expert, and the civic expert, which

I adopted from Brand and Karvonen (2007, 26–9). I further proposed that we should add a fifth type of mediating expert, which I labeled the political expert.

In Chapter 5, I offered a sixth contribution, namely four criteria for the selection of capabilities for human development purposes. The four criteria—methodological justification, normative justification, democratic legitimacy, and contextual sensitivity—provide a basis for formulating and/or evaluating future development agendas.

Finally, in Chapter 6, I provided the first comprehensive overview, analysis, and evaluation of fifteen methods for the selection of capabilities proposed within the capability literature. While the issue of selecting capabilities has traditionally been seen as a choice between foundational or philosophical approaches to identifying normatively relevant capabilities on the one hand and procedural or democratic methods on the other hand, the chapter broadens the scope of possible methods and shows the advantages and disadvantages of applying each to the context of selecting capabilities for development purposes. The analyses of Chapter 6 may also be useful beyond the development context, however, and may provide a useful basis for capability theorists to choose a method for the selection of capabilities in other domains of research.

In sum, the book and its individual chapters offer several novel discussions and concepts that contribute to the development literature and to development practice. Some of these might also be relevant beyond the limited scope of setting development agendas. In the following section, I consider how the book can contribute to other debates and what opportunities for future research that it presents.

7.4 Evaluating the MDGs and SDGs

I began this book by claiming that one of the most important tasks of development is the setting of a development agenda that identifies the goals that development should aim to achieve. Two of the most influential global development agendas are the MDGs and their successors the SDGs. Given that this book was in large part motivated by the democratic shortcomings of the MDGs, it is only natural at this point to attempt to evaluate the SDGs based on the three-part framework that I set out in the previous chapters.

The first thing we should notice about both the MDGs and the SDGs, however, is their political purpose. That is, the primary aim of these development agendas was not to provide a non-question-begging, fully justified list of development goals, but rather to thrust development issues back into the global spotlight. Through the 1990s, development had all but vanished from the global political agenda out of discontent with the progress being made, and development aid had been on the decline (Fukuda-Parr 2012, 13–15; Fukuda-Parr and Hulme 2011). While several attempts had been made to set out a set of goals—most significantly the International Development Targets (IDTs; OECD 1996)—these had all but failed to unite world leaders and the international development community around a global action plan for development and poverty alleviation. The issue with these attempts, such as the IDTs, was as Fukuda-Parr (2012, 14) argues that the goals "could not be 'owned' by all stakeholders since they were invented by the bilateral donors."

However, the traction that the IDTs had gained by setting out a simple and effective list of six goals within three areas—economic well-being, social development, and environmental sustainability and regeneration (OECD 1996, 1–2)—inspired the United Nations to include concrete goals in the outcome document—popularly referred to as the *Millennium Declaration*—of the Millennium Summit in Paris in 2000 (United Nations 2000; Fukuda-Parr 2012, 14–15). The MDGs, which aimed to summarize the commitments of the *Millennium Declaration* into a concrete list of goals, were revealed one year later in a report from the UN Secretary-General (United Nations 2001; Fukuda-Parr 2012, 1). Consequently, the implementation of the MDGs can best be described as an attempt to save the *Millennium Declaration*, which set out the commitments that would be represented by the MDGs, from falling into oblivion like so many of its predecessors.

One of the main problems with the MDGs was the lack of possibility for democratic participation and input from civil society, especially from the developing world, in the design and implementation process of the MDGs. As both Hall et al. (2013, 6) and Wisor (2012, 119) note, the formulation, adoption, and implementation of the MDGs was largely a donor-driven process that paid little attention to the preferences of developing countries and NGOs.[1] The MDGs, so to speak, was an attempt to thrust development back into the global political agenda without the constraints of political consensus. As Wisor (2012, 120) puts it, "[t]he MDGs were snuck in the back door at the United Nations, allowing their architects to sidestep normal discussion and voting."

In short, the procedure surrounding the formulation and adoption of the MDGs suffered from three democratic shortcomings, namely the lack of transparency, feedback, and deliberation (Wisor 2012, 119–20). That is, there was little to no opportunity for stakeholders to gain insight into the selection of the concrete targets, benchmarks, and indicators or to object to them. The MDGs, to put it bluntly, *imposed* a set of global development goals on countries, which were already disadvantaged in terms of their capacities to achieve these goals. More importantly, in addition to imposing a set of goals, which were insensitive to the socioeconomic contexts of the developing countries, the lack of democratic participation by developing countries and local communities in the formulation and implementation of the MDGs meant that they lacked any ownership of the new development agenda that the MDGs reflected. In the meantime, however, many developing countries have shed their donor-dependency (Hall et al. 2013, 6).

Given the political purpose of the MDGs—that is, to put development back on the global agenda—it is difficult to fault their authors for not living up to the democratic requirements set out by the second and third parts of the framework presented in this book. By presenting a limited list of development goals, the MDGs have been hugely successful in making development a global priority.

The SDGs, however, were intended to address many of these procedural shortcomings of the MDGs. Replacing the MDGs, the SDGs expand the set of goals from eight to 18 with 169 specific targets, constituting 304 indicators, to be achieved by 2030 (United Nations 2015). New commitments, compared to the MDGs, include specific goals related, among others, to energy, infrastructure, habitation, marine ecosystems, and institutions. The initiative to the SDGs was taken at the United Nations Conference on Sustainable Development in Rio de Janeiro in 2012 (popularly referred to as Rio+20 to indicate the 20-year anniversary of the 1992 UN Conference on Environment and Development, also held in Rio). Although no specific goals were adopted at Rio+20, the UN General Assembly decided to task a 30-member[2] so-called Open Working Group (OWG) with the responsibility of preparing a proposal for a post-2013 development agenda (United Nations 2012, 2013).

In many ways, the process that the OWG undertook promised to rectify the procedural shortcomings of the MDGs. As such, the OWG was committed to engage a broader range of stakeholders in the consultation process, "including major groups, civil society, scientific and knowledge institutions, parliaments, local authorities, and the private sector" (United Nations 2014). Importantly, the process was informed by survey data on the values of almost 10 million people around the world,[3] signifying an improved commitment to securing the democratic legitimacy of the goals.

To what extent, then, do the SDGs meet the criteria for a justifiable development agenda as set out in this book? The first question we need to ask is, are the SDGs formulated in terms of the capability framework that I develop in Chapter 2? The SDGs are multi-dimensional goals, and some of them are formulated in terms of providing substantive opportunities. This is, for example, the case of SDG4 ("[e]nsure inclusive and equitable quality education and promote lifelong learning opportunities for all" (United Nations 2015, 17)), SDG7 ("access to affordable, reliable, sustainable and modern energy for all" (United Nations 2015, 19)), and SDG11 (ensure that urban populations have access to safe and affordable housing, transport systems, and public spaces (United Nations 2015, 21–2)). SDG12 stresses the functioning of sustainable consumption and production.

Many of the goals, however, are formulated less as opportunities but rather in terms of the *means* for (sustainable) development. For example,

SDG2 aims to end hunger, SDG9 is focused on promoting sustainable growth, and SDG14 and SDG15 are focused on preserving biodiversity in the oceans and on land. Although these factors are important for having capabilities, they do not as such identify what capabilities that people should have. As such, they merely state the means, rather than the ends, of development.

The second question that we need to ask is whether, or to what extent, the SDGs respect local political and expert authority in matters of development. The first thing we should notice is that by implementing a consultancy process that sought the advice of a diverse set of stakeholders, the SDGs certainly constitute an improvement over the MDGs in this regard. Through the consultancy process, the authors of the SDGs did include representatives of civil society and local authorities, indicating that a respect for the expert authority of local stakeholders, while the survey of what kinds of goals that people value sought to ensure some level of democratic legitimacy for the goals.

It is not clear, however, whether this survey constitutes a respect for the local political authority as set out by the republican account developed in Chapter 3. Recall that although local political authority does not require that local stakeholders outright choose the goals, it does require that the goals represent what they would have chosen had they had the opportunity. The question, thus, is to what extent the actual goals are adequately representative of the values expressed by local stakeholders: how much did the survey of values influence the actual SDGs?

To a large extent, the answer to this question hinges on how we answer the third question asked in this book: what method was ultimately used to formulate the SDGs? There is little doubt that some kind of multi-stage method was used in this regard. If we consider how the MDGs were grounded in a normative view of development, by building on the MDGs, the authors of the SDGs partly make use of a foundational methodology. Yet whereas the MDGs fail to supplement this foundational approach with a procedural approach, the SDGs also include at least two procedural methods, namely a consultancy process and the value survey. The question, then, is whether this multi-stage process by which the SDGs were formulated constitutes the comparative method or the synthesizing method.

Recall that in Chapter 6 I argued that a synthesizing method would be preferable for setting a justifiable development agenda. What distinguishes the synthesizing method from the comparative method is that whereas the comparative method starts out from idealized list of goals, which is then specified through a procedural exercise, the synthesizing method engages in a critical and dialectical 'conversation' between goals derived from the foundational and procedural methods. If this is how the two multi-stage methods are distinguished, it seems that the process by which the SDGs were formulated does go beyond merely comparing lists of development goals to actively employ a synthesizing approach. Although the survey of values can be seen as merely an effort to enrich, refine, and supplement the normative view of development left over from the MDGs, the SDG process additionally invokes a procedural methodology—namely consultations with stakeholders—to provide a critical view of the MDGs and how they could be improved. This conforms to the three-step procedure of synthesizing methods, moving from (1) theory (i.e., the MDGs) to (2) practice (i.e., the consultancy process and, partly, the survey of values) to (3) a synthesis (i.e., the SDGs).

In sum, this exercise in how to apply the framework developed in this book to evaluate an existing development agenda shows how the SDGs in many ways conform to the framework for setting a justifiable development agenda that I have set out in this book. To be sure, setting a development agenda according to this framework, which puts a lot of weight on being procedural, is an ongoing process that requires continued evaluation and refinement. Thus, the SDGs are not and *should* not be immune to critiques. Indeed, in the wake of their adoption, many scholars have highlighted shortcomings of the SDGs, such their lack of conceptual clarity; the lack of concrete measurable outcomes and deadlines; their unrealistic ambitions; the lack of consistency in regard to whether the goals are global, regional, or national; the lack of interconnectivity between goals; and the lack of commitment to institutional reform (De Fraia 2015; Dunning and Elgin-Cossart 2015; Fan and Polman 2014; ICSU and ISSC 2015; Kerr 2015; Lloyd-Sherlock 2015; Pogge and Sengupta 2015; Sengupta 2016; Stewart 2015; Vandemoortele 2015a, 2015b, 2015c; Waldmueller 2015). Many of these criticisms will provide an important input when the SDGs will need to be revised in 2030.

7.5 Beyond a Development Agenda

While the initial motivation of this book has concerned the question of how to advance toward a democratic, sustainable, inclusive, and integrated development agenda, I contend that the analyses and conclusions have additional relevance. This is so both in relation to other development discussions and to other related domains. Because these additional applications have not been discussed in the main chapters, let me by way of conclusion briefly consider how the overall framework of this book as well as the more particular answers to the three questions can be applied beyond the context of a development agenda.

First, the framework for the selection of capabilities and functionings that I set out in this book can be applied whenever we need to consider what the aims of development are or should be—whether at a local, national, regional, or global level, and whether in a short- or long-term perspective. That is, as has been a constant theme throughout this book, identifying normatively relevant capabilities and functionings provides

(a) the goals that development initiatives and policies should strive to achieve and (b) a basis on which we can evaluate the performance of these development initiatives and policies. As such, the framework does not necessarily concern itself with a global development agenda but can be adapted to the design of more locally oriented development projects or national development policies.

Hence, when developing new development initiatives or policies, we may proactively adopt the framework that I have detailed in this book, either wholesale or in part. For example, we may insist that a development policy should aim at expanding people's capabilities yet should not include them in the process of identifying the relevant dimensions. Likewise, we may have a strong commitment to involve local stakeholders early in the process of designing a development project yet adopt one of the other methods for selecting relevant capabilities and functionings. I hope, however, that I have provided convincing arguments for why the framework should be adopted as a collected set of normative commitments for the proactive identification of development goals.

However, as Alkire's (2002) three case studies make clear, it is not always possible to determine the positive or negative consequences of a development initiative in advance. Sometimes it is only possible in retrospect to identify what should have been the normatively relevant capabilities and functionings by which the initiative should have been evaluated. However, I contend that my framework can also be applied to such retrospective and evaluative exercises—so-called monitoring and evaluation (M&E) or, more recently, monitoring, evaluation, accountability, and learning (MEAL) exercises. M&E/MEAL exercises are crucial within development practices because they ensure that development initiatives do not become static and are adaptable to changing circumstances and new insights.[4]

The framework presented in this book can also be adopted for and adapted to the monitoring and evaluation of the performance of development agendas and the subsequent development initiatives and policies. For example, the idea that development should be concerned with the expansion of certain capabilities and functionings is also relevant for the evaluation of development progress, while a republican conception of local political authority highlights the need to make international development organizations accountable to local development stakeholders.

As such, adopting my framework means that local stakeholders should be involved in the monitoring and evaluation process, for example by deliberating with them about how the initiative or policy has affected their lives (both positively and negatively) or what changes they would like to see made. Granted, there may be differences between the prospective approach taken in this book and the retrospective approach needed for monitoring and evaluation that need to be taken into account. How the framework of this book can be adapted to M&E/MEAL exercises and what challenges are presented in the process should be a subject for further research.

Moreover, in this book I have talked about development in general and have refrained from discussing particular development contexts and issues other than by way of example. The general framework that I have presented here—including the three normative commitments—may also require further specification when applied to particular development contexts and issues, such as climate change or future generations.

Both of these contexts raise questions about who counts as an agent of development, for example. In the first case, addressing climate change may require the imposing of restrictions on one set of local stakeholders (i.e., in developed countries) in order to ensure the continued survival or well-being of another set of local stakeholders (e.g., inhabitants of Small Island Developing States). With our commitment to granting local stakeholders more authority, applying the framework to address climate change issues requires a consideration of how to solve this tension. The second case concerns how to represent future generations in current discussions about development. Again, a tension may exist between what levels of development current generations may wish to achieve, on the one hand, and not knowing what levels of development future generations may wish to achieve, on the other. Again, how the general framework can be applied to such specific contexts and what challenges it poses, must be a subject for further research.

Finally, many of the arguments presented in this book may apply to domains other than development. For example, the defense of local political authority in Chapter 3 may be applicable to democratic governance in general, while the concept of third wave expertise may be more generally valid within scientific discussions. The synthesizing method developed in Chapter 6 can also be adapted within other contexts, such as health-care ethics, and although the four criteria are tailored to the issue of human development, they may prove to be a useful starting point for setting out similar criteria within other domains, like I did with Robeyns's (2003) set of criteria.

7.6 Concluding Remarks

In conclusion, this book sets out three normative claims—(a) that development goals should be conceptualized in terms of capabilities and functionings, (b) that the process should include a variety of stakeholders, not least local stakeholders, and (c) that the method used should aim to engage in a critical dialogue with local stakeholders—that have an impact within development, both in general and in relation to the setting of a development agenda in particular, as well as potentially within other domains of public decision-making and their academic counterparts, such as health-care ethics, distributive justice, gender equality, and so on. Thus, while the focus here has been on how to set out a development agenda, the discussions, arguments, and concepts that I have developed in this context may inspire and foster further research projects, both within and outside of development.

I set out my ambition for this book in the introduction, and I hope that I have provided a compelling framework for identifying development goals for future development agendas or at the very least have encouraged development stakeholders—donors, experts, practitioners, and policy-makers—to carefully consider what they mean when they talk about development.

Notes

1 Why did the developing countries, after all, support the implementation of the Development Declaration and the MDGs despite their flaws? As Fukuda-Parr (2012, 15) explains, "the priority for the developing countries was to keep the development issue a high priority on the UN agenda, on part with political issues," and the aim of the MDGs was to do exactly that.
2 Most of the seats of the Open Working Group were shared between several member states. Algeria, Egypt, Morocco, and Tunisia, for example, shared their membership.
3 See http://data.myworld2015.org/.
4 For an influential introduction to monitoring and evaluation in development, see Kusek and Rist (2004).

Bibliography

Agrawal, Arun. 1995a. "Dismantling the Divide Between Indigenous and Scientific Knowledge." *Development and Change* 26:413.

———. 1995b. "Indigenous and Scientific Knowledge: Some Critical Comments." *Development and Change* 26 (3):413–39.

Alexander, John M. 2004. "Capabilities, Human Rights and Moral Pluralism." *International Journal of Human Rights* 8 (4):451–69.

Alkire, Sabina. 2002. *Valuing Freedoms: Sen's Capability Approach and Poverty Reduction*. Oxford: Oxford University Press.

———. 2008. "Choosing Dimensions: The Capability Approach and Multidimensional Poverty." MPRA Working Papers No. 8862.

Alkire, Sabina, and Séverine Deneulin. 2009. "A Normative Framework for Development." In *An Introduction to the Human Development Capability Approach*, edited by Séverine Deneulin and Lila Shahani. London: Earthscan.

Alkire, Sabina, and James Foster. 2011. "Counting and Multidimensional Poverty Measurement." *Journal of Public Economics* 95 (7):476–87.

Alsop, Ruth, Mette Frost Bertelsen, and Jeremy Holland. 2006. *Empowerment in Practice: From Analysis to Implementation*. Washington, DC: World Bank.

Anderson, Elizabeth. 1999. "What Is the Point of Equality?" *Ethics* 109 (2):287–337.

———. 2003. "Sen, Ethics, and Democracy." *Feminist Economics* 9 (2–3):239–61.

Argenton, Carlo, and Enzo Rossi. 2013. "Pluralism, Preferences, and Deliberation: A Critique of Sen's Constructive Argument for Democracy." *Journal of Social Philosophy* 44 (2):129–45.

Arneson, Richard. 2006. "Distributive Justice and Basic Capability Equality." In *Capabilities Equality: Basic Issues and Problems*, edited by Alexander Kaufman, 17–43. New York and London: Routledge.

Astroulakis, Nikos. 2011. "The Development Ethics Approach to International Development." *International Journal of Development Issues* 10 (3):214–32.

Ballon, Paola. 2013. *The Selection of Functionings and Capabilities: A Survey of Empirical Studies*. Nairobi: Partnership for Economic Policy (PEP).

Barcham, Manuhuia. 2012. "Thinking About Maori Development in Terms of the Capability Approach." In *The Capability Approach. Development Practice and Public Policy in the Asia-Pacific Region*, edited by Francesca Panzironi and Katharine Gelber, 55–67. London: Routledge.

Barclay, Linda. 2003. "What Kind of Liberal Is Martha Nussbaum?" *SATS—Nordic Journal of Philosophy* 4 (2):5–24.

Barr, Abigail, and David Clark. 2009. "Do the Poor Adapt to Low Income, Minimal Education and Ill-Health?" *Journal of African Economies* 19 (3):257–93.

Basu, K. 1987. "Achievements, Capabilities and the Concept of Well-Being." *Social Choice and Welfare* 4 (1):69–76.

Beck, Tony, and Madan G. Ghosh. 2000. "Common Property Resources and the Poor: Findings from West Bengal." *Economic and Political Weekly* 35 (3):147–53.

Berlin, Isaiah. 1969. *Four Essays on Liberty*. Oxford: Oxford University Press.

Bicchieri, Cristina, and Annalisa Marini. 2015. "Female Genital Mutilation: Fundamentals, Social Expectations and Change." MPRA Paper.

Biggeri, Mario, Renato Libanora, Stefano Mariani, and Leonardo Menchini. 2006. "Children Conceptualizing Their Capabilities: Results of a Survey Conducted During the First Children's World Congress on Child Labour." *Journal of Human Development* 7 (1):59–83.

Binder, Christina, and Constanze Binder. 2016. "A Capability Perspective on Indigenous Autonomy." *Oxford Development Studies* 44 (3): 297–314.

Bingle, Wade H., and P. James Gaskell. 1994. "Scientific Literacy for Decision-making and the Social Construction of Scientific Knowledge." *Science Education* 78 (2):185–201.

Birn, Anne-Emanuelle. 2014. "Philanthrocapitalism, Past and Present: The Rockefeller Foundation, the Gates Foundation, and the Setting(s) of the International/Global Health Agenda." *Hypothesis* 12 (1):1–27.

Bohman, James. 1997. "Deliberative Democracy and Effective Social Freedom: Capabilities, Resources, and Opportunities." In *Deliberative Democracy: Essays on Reason and Politics*, edited by James Bohman and William Rehg, 321–48. Cambridge, MA: MIT Press.

———. 2012. "Critical Theory, Republicanism, and the Priority of Injustice: Transnational Republicanism as a Nonideal Theory." *Journal of Social Philosophy* 43 (2):97–112.

Bollig, Michael, and Anja Schulte. 1999. "Environmental Change and Pastoral Perceptions: Degradation and Indigenous Knowledge in Two African Pastoral Communities." *Human Ecology* 27 (3):493–514.

Bowman, Andrew. 2012. "The Flip Side to Bill Gates' Charity Billions." *New Internationalist*, April 12, 2012. http://newint.org/features/2012/04/01/bill-gates-charitable-giving-ethics/.

Bradshaw, Ted K., and Edward J. Blakely. 1999. "What Are 'Third-Wave' State Economic Development Efforts? From Incentives to Industrial Policy." *Economic Development Quarterly* 13 (3):229–44.

Brand, Ralf, and Andrew Karvonen. 2007. "The Ecosystem of Expertise: Complementary Knowledges for Sustainable Development." *Sustainability: Science, Practice, & Policy* 3 (1):21–31.

Briggs, John. 2005. "The Use of Indigenous Knowledge in Development: Problems and Challenges." *Progress in Development Studies* 5 (2):99–114.

Brock, Gillian. 2009. *Global Justice : A Cosmopolitan Account*. Oxford: Oxford University Press.

Bucchi, Massimiano. 2009. *Beyond Technocracy: Science, Politics and Citizens*. New York: Springer.

Burchardt, Tania, and Polly Vizard. 2011. " 'Operationalising' the Capability Approach as a Basis for Equality and Human Rights Monitoring in 21st

Century Britain." In *Human Rights and the Capabilities Approach: An Interdisciplinary Dialogue*, edited by Diane Elson, Sakiko Fukuda-Parr, and Polly Vizard. London: Routledge.

Byskov, Morten Fibieger. 2017a. "Democracy, Philosophy, and the Selection of Capabilities." *Journal of Human Development and Capabilities* 18 (1):1–16.

———. 2017b. "Third Wave Development Expertise." *Oxford Development Studies* 45 (3):352–65.

Carter, Ian. 2012. "Positive and Negative Liberty." In *The Stanford Encyclopedia of Philosophy*, edited by Edward N. Zalta, Spring. http://plato.stanford.edu/archives/spr2012/entries/liberty-positive-negative/.

———. 2014. "Is the Capability Approach Paternalist?" *Economics & Philosophy* 30 (1):75–98.

Cash, David W., W. Neil Adger, Fikret Berkes, Po Garden, Louis Lebel, Per Olsson, Lowell Pritchard, and Oran Young. 2006. "Scale and Cross-Scale Dynamics: Governance and Information in a Multilevel World." *Ecology and Society* 11 (2):8.

Centers for Disease Control and Prevention. 1999. *Achievements in Public Health, 1900–1999: Healthier Mothers and Babies*. Atlanta, GA: Centers for Disease Control and Prevention.

Chambers, Robert. 1995. "Poverty and Livelihoods: Whose Reality Counts?" *Environment and Urbanization* 7 (1):173–204.

———. 1997. *Whose Reality Counts? Putting the First Last*. London: Intermediate Technology.

Christiano, Thomas. 2010. "The Uneasy Relationship between Democracy and Capital." *Social Philosophy & Policy* 27 (1):195–217.

———. 2012. "Money in Politics." In *The Oxford Handbook of Political Philosophy*, edited by David Estlund, 241–60. Oxford: Oxford University Press.

Claassen, Rutger. 2011. "Making Capability Lists: Philosophy Versus Democracy." *Political Studies* 59 (3):491–508.

———. 2014. "Capability Paternalism." *Economics & Philosophy* 30 (1):57–73.

Claassen, Rutger, and Marcus Düwell. 2013. "The Foundations of Capability Theory: Comparing Nussbaum and Gewirth." *Ethical Theory and Moral Practice* 16 (3):493–510.

Clark, David A. 2002. *Visions of Development. A Study of Human Values*. Cheltenham, UK: Edward Elgar Publishing.

———. 2005. "Sen's Capability Approach and the Many Spaces of Human Well-Being." *Journal of Development Studies* 41 (8):1339–60.

———. 2009. "Adaptation, Poverty and Well-Being: Some Issues and Observations with Special Reference to the Capability Approach and Development Studies." *Journal of Human Development and Capabilities* 10 (1):21–42.

Clark, David A., and Mozaffar Qizilbash. 2008. "Core Poverty, Vagueness and Adaptation: A New Methodology and Some Results for South Africa." *Journal of Development Studies* 44 (4):519–44.

Cohen, G. A. 2003. "Facts and Principles." *Philosophy & Public Affairs* 31 (3):211–45.

Cole, Stephen. 1992. *Making Science: Between Nature and Society*. Cambridge, MA: Harvard University Press.

Collins, Harry, and Robert Evans. 2002. "The Third Wave of Science Studies: Studies of Expertise and Experience." *Social Studies of Science* 32 (2):235–96.

———. 2008. *Rethinking Expertise*. Chicago: University of Chicago Press.
Comim, Flavio. 2008. "Measuring Capabilities." In *The Capability Approach: Concepts, Measures and Applications*, edited by Flavio Comim, Mozaffar Qizilbash, and Sabina Alkire, 157–200. Cambridge, UK: Cambridge University Press.
Conradie, Ina, and Ingrid Robeyns. 2013. "Aspirations and Human Development Interventions." *Journal of Human Development and Capabilities* 14 (4):559–80.
Cooke, Bill. 2003. "A New Continuity with Colonial Administration: Participation in Development Management." *Third World Quarterly* 24 (1):47–61.
———. 2004. "The Managing of the (Third) World." *Organization* 11 (5):603–29.
Cooke, Bill, and Uma Kothari. 2001. *Participation: The New Tyranny?* London: Zed Books.
Costa, M. Victoria. 2007. "Freedom as Non-Domination, Normativity, and Indeterminacy." *Journal of Value Inquiry* 41 (2–4):291–307.
Crabtree, Andrew. 2013. "Sustainable Development: Does the Capability Approach Have Anything to Offer? Outlining a Legitimate Freedom Approach." *Journal of Human Development and Capabilities* 14 (1):40–57.
Crabtree, Andrew, and Meera Tiwari. forthcoming. *Capability and Sustainability*. Palgrave Macmillan.
Craig, David, and Doug Porter. 2003. "Poverty Reduction Strategy Papers: A New Convergence." *World Development* 31 (1):53–69.
Credit Suisse. 2013. *Global Wealth Report 2013*. Zurich: Credit Suisse.
Crocker, David A. 1991. "Toward Development Ethics." *World Development* 19 (5):457–83.
———. 2005. "8 Sen and Deliberative Democracy." In *Capabilities Equality: Basic Issues and Problems*, edited by Alexander Kaufman, 155. New York: Routledge.
———. 2008. *Ethics of Global Development: Agency, Capability, and Deliberative Democracy*. Cambridge: Cambridge University Press.
Crocker, David A., and Ingrid Robeyns. 2010. "Capability and Agency." In *Amartya Sen*, edited by Christopher Morris, 60–90. Cambridge: Cambridge University Press.
Dagger, Richard. 2006. "Neo-Republicanism and the Civic Economy." *Politics, Philosophy & Economics* 5 (2):151–73.
Davis, Diana K. 2005. "Indigenous Knowledge and the Desertification Debate: Problematising Expert Knowledge in North Africa." *Geoforum* 36 (4):509–24.
De Fraia, Luca. 2015. "Will the Post-2015 Agenda Support Country Ownership of Sustainable Development Processes?" *Post2015.Org—What Comes After the MDGs?* (blog). http://post2015.org/2015/07/02/will-the-post-2015-agenda-support-country-ownership-of-sustainable-development-processes/.
Deneulin, Séverine. 2002. "Perfectionism, Paternalism and Liberalism in Sen and Nussbaum's Capability Approach." *Review of Political Economy* 14 (4):497–518.
Deneulin, Séverine, and Ana C. Dinerstein. 2010. *Hope Movements: Social Movements in the Pursuit of Human Development*. Working Paper 8. Bath, UK: Centre for Development Studies, University of Bath.
DeWalt, Billie. 1994. "Using Indigenous Knowledge to Improve Agriculture and Natural Resource Management." *Human Organization* 53 (2):123–31.

Di Tommaso, Maria Laura. 2007. “Children Capabilities: A Structural Equation Model for India.” *Journal of Socio-Economics* 36 (3):436–50.

Dixon, Rosalind, Martha Nussbaum, Beverly Baines, Daphne Barak-Erez, and Tsvi Kahana. 2011. “Abortion, Dignity and a Capabilities Approach.” Public Law and Legal Theory Working Papers No. 345.

Doyal, Len and Ian Gough. 1991. *A Theory of Human Needs*. New York: Palgrave Macmillan.

Drèze, Jean, and Amartya Sen. 2002. “Democratic Practice and Social Inequality in India.” *Journal of Asian and African Studies* 37 (2):6–37.

Drydyk, Jay. 2005. “When Is Development More Democratic?” *Journal of Human Development* 6 (2):247–67.

———. 2008. “Durable Empowerment.” *Journal of Global Ethics* 4 (3):231–45.

———. 2011. “Responsible Pluralism, Capabilities, and Human Rights.” *Journal of Human Development and Capabilities* 12 (1):39–61.

———. 2013. “Empowerment, Agency, and Power.” *Journal of Global Ethics* 9 (3):249–62.

Dunning, Casey, and Molly Elgin-Cossart. 2015. “Can the SDGs Really ‘Leave No One Behind’?” *Post2015.Org—What Comes After the MDGs?* (blog). http://post2015.org/2015/07/03/can-the-sdgs-really-leave-no-one-behind/.

Easterly, William. 2013. *The Tyranny of Experts: Economists, Dictators, and the Forgotten Rights of the Poor*. New York: Basic Books.

Edwards, Arthur. 1999. “Scientific Expertise and Policy-Making: The Intermediary Role of the Public Sphere.” *Science and Public Policy* 26 (3):163–70.

Epstein, Steven. 1995. “The Construction of Lay Expertise: AIDS Activism and the Forging of Credibility in the Reform of Clinical Trials.” *Science, Technology & Human Values* 20 (4):408–37.

———. 1996. *Impure Science: AIDS, Activism, and the Politics of Knowledge*. Berkeley: University of California Press.

Fan, Shenggen, and Paul Polman. 2014. *An Ambitious Development Goal: Ending Hunger and Undernutrition by 2025*. In *2013 Global Food Report*, edited by Andrew Marble and Heidi Fritschel, 15–28. Washington, D.C.: International Food Policy Research Institute.

Ferguson, James. 1990. *The Anti-Politics Machine: “Development,” Depoliticization, and Bureaucratic Power in Lesotho*. Minneapolis: University of Minnesota Press.

———. 1994. “The Anti-Politics Machine.” *Ecologist* 24 (5):176–81.

Ferracioli, Luara, and Rosa Terlazzo. 2014. “Educating for Autonomy: Liberalism and Autonomy in the Capabilities Approach.” *Ethical Theory and Moral Practice* 17 (3):443–55.

Fleurbaey, Marc. 2006. “Capabilities, Functionings and Refined Functionings.” *Journal of Human Development* 7 (3):299–310.

Frankfurt, Harry G. 1971. “Freedom of the Will and the Concept of a Person.” *The Journal of Philosophy* 64 (1): 5–20.

Frediani, Alexandre Apsan. 2007. “A Participatory Approach to Choosing Dimensions.” *Maitreyee, e-Bulletin of the Human Development and Capability Association* 7:7–10.

Fricker, Miranda. 2007. *Epistemic Injustice: Power and the Ethics of Knowing*. Oxford: Oxford University Press.

Fukuda-Parr, Sakiko. 2003. "Rescuing the Human Development Concept from the HDI—Reflections on a New Agenda." In *Readings in Human Development*, edited by Sakiko Fukuda-Parr and A. K. Shiva Kumar, 93–100. New Delhi: Oxford University Press.

———. 2011. "The Metrics of Human Rights: Complementarities of the Human Development and Capabilities Approach." *Journal of Human Development and Capabilities* 12 (1):73–89.

———. 2012. "Should Global Goal Setting Continue, and How, in the Post-2015 Era?" SSRN Scholarly Paper ID 2211566. Rochester, NY: Social Science Research Network.

Fukuda-Parr, Sakiko, and David Hulme. 2011. "International Norm Dynamics and the 'End of Poverty': Understanding the Millennium Development Goals." *Global Governance: A Review of Multilateralism and International Organizations* 17 (1):17–36.

Funtowicz, Silvio O., and Jerome R. Ravetz. 1991. "A New Scientific Methodology for Global Environmental Issues." In *Ecological Economics: The Science and Management of Sustainability*, edited by Robert Costanza, 137–52. New York: Columbia University Press.

Gasper, Des. 2002. "Is Sen's Capability Approach an Adequate Basis for Considering Human Development?" *Review of Political Economy* 14 (4):435–61.

———. 2005. "Securing Humanity: Situating 'Human Security' as Concept and Discourse." *Journal of Human Development* 6 (2):221–45.

Gasper, Des, and Thanh-Dam Truong. 2005. "Deepening Development Ethics: From Economism to Human Development to Human Security." *European Journal of Development Research* 17 (3):372–84.

———. 2008. "Development Ethics Through the Lenses of Caring, Gender, and Human Security." *ISS Working Paper Series/General Series* 459 (September):1–37.

Gewirth, Alan. 1978. *Reason and Morality*. Chicago: University of Chicago Press.

———. 1996. *The Community of Rights*. Chicago: University of Chicago Press.

Gilabert, Pablo. 2011. "Feasibility and Socialism." *Journal of Political Philosophy* 19 (1):52–63.

Gilroy, Rose. 2007. "Taking a Capabilities Approach to Evaluating Supportive Environments for Older People." *Applied Research in Quality of Life* 1 (3–4):343–56.

Goulet, Denis. 1971. *The Cruel Choice: A New Concept in the Theory of Development*. New York: Atheneum.

Habermas, Jürgen. 1989. *The Structural Transformation of the Public Sphere*. Cambridge: Polity Press.

———. 1996. *Between Facts and Norms: Contributions to a Discourse Theory of Law and Democracy*. Cambridge: Polity Press.

Hall, Jon, Christina Hackmann, Rolph van der Hoeven, and James Heintz. 2013. *Issues for a Global Human Development Agenda*. New York: UNDP.

Haq, Mahbub ul. 1996. *Reflections on Human Development*. New York: Oxford University Press.

Hering-Hanit, R., and N. Gadoth. 2003. "Caffeine-Induced Headache in Children and Adolescents." *Cephalalgia* 23 (5):332–35.

Hickman, Larry A. 1992. "Populism and the Cult of the Expert." In *Democracy in a Technological Society*, edited by Langdon Winner, 91–103. Dordrecht: Kluwer Academic.

Hobbes, Thomas. 1991. *Leviathan*. Edited by Richard Tuck. Cambridge: Cambridge University Press.

Hodgett, Susan, and Séverine Deneulin. 2009. "On the Use of Narratives for Assessing Development Policy." *Public Administration* 87 (1):65–79.

Holland, Breena. 2008. "Ecology and the Limits of Justice: Establishing Capability Ceilings in Nussbaum's Capabilities Approach." *Journal of Human Development* 9 (3):401–25.

———. 2014. *Allocating the Earth: A Distributional Framework for Protecting Capabilities in Environmental Law and Policy*. Oxford: Oxford University Press.

Hu, Frank B., and Vasanti S. Malik. 2010. "Sugar-Sweetened Beverages and Risk of Obesity and Type 2 Diabetes: Epidemiologic Evidence." *Physiology & Behavior*, Beverages and Health, 100 (1):47–54.

Huber, Evelyne, Dietrich Rueschemeyer, and John D. Stephens. 1997. "The Paradoxes of Contemporary Democracy: Formal, Participatory, and Social Dimensions." *Comparative Politics* 29 (3):323–42.

Ibrahim, Solava. 2011. "Poverty, Aspirations and Well-Being: Afraid to Aspire and Unable to Reach a Better Life—Voices from Egypt." SSRN Scholarly Paper ID 1747798. Rochester, NY: Social Science Research Network.

ICSU and ISSC. 2015. *Review of Targets for the Sustainable Development Goals: The Science Perspective*. Paris: International Council for Science (ICSU).

International Programme on the Elimination of Child Labour (IPEC). 2013. *Marking Progress against Child Labour. Global Estimates and Trends 2000–2012*. Geneva: International Labour Organization.

IPCC. 2014. *Climate Change 2014: Impacts, Adaptation, and Vulnerability*. Cambridge: Cambridge University Press.

Irwin, Alan, and Brian Wynne. 2003. *Misunderstanding Science? The Public Reconstruction of Science and Technology*. New York: Cambridge University Press.

Jaggar, Alison M. 2006. "Reasoning About Well-Being: Nussbaum's Methods of Justifying the Capabilities." *Journal of Political Philosophy* 14 (3):301–22.

Jasanoff, Sheila. 1987. "Contested Boundaries in Policy-Relevant Science." *Social Studies of Science* 17 (2):195–230.

———. 2004. *States of Knowledge: The Co-Production of Science and the Social Order*. New York: Routledge.

Katz, Stanley N. 2005. "What Does It Mean to Say That Philanthropy Is 'Effective'? The Philanthropists' New Clothes." *Proceedings of the American Philosophical Society* 149 (2):123–31.

Keene, Courtney. 2007. *Development Projects That Didn't Work*. New York: Globalhood, Inc.

Kerr, Laura. 2015. "Leaving No One behind: Realism vs Optimism in Kenya." *Post2015.Org—What Comes After the MDGs?* (blog). http://post2015.org/2015/08/06/leaving-no-one-behind-realism-vs-optimism-in-kenya/.

Khader, Serene J. 2009. "Adaptive Preferences and Procedural Autonomy." *Journal of Human Development and Capabilities* 10 (2):169–87.

———. 2011. *Adaptive Preferences and Women's Empowerment*. New York: Oxford University Press.

———. 2013. "Identifying Adaptive Preferences in Practice: Lessons from Postcolonial Feminisms." *Journal of Global Ethics* 9 (3):311–27.

Klasen, Stephen. 2000. "Measuring Poverty and Deprivation in South Africa." *Review of Income and Wealth* 46 (1):33–58.

Kleinman, Daniel Lee. 2000. "Democratizations of Science and Technology." In *Science, Technology, and Democracy*, edited by Daniel Lee Kleinman, 139–63. Albany: State University of New York Press.

Knight, Frank Hyneman. 1982. *Freedom and Reform: Essays in Economics and Social Philosophy*. Indianapolis: Liberty Press.

Koehler, Gabriele, Des Gasper, Richard Jolly, and Mara Simane. 2012. *Human Security and the Next Generation of Comprehensive Development Goals*. Brighton: Institute of Development Studies.

Kramer, Mark R. 2002. "Will Venture Philanthropy Leave a Lasting Mark on Charitable Giving." *Chronicle of Philanthropy*, May 2, 2002.

Kriegel, Blandine. 1995. *The State and the Rule of Law*. Princeton, NJ: Princeton University Press.

Krishnakumar, Jaya. 2007. "Going beyond Functionings and Capabilities: An Econometric Model to Explain and Estimate Capabilities." *Journal of Human Development* 8 (1):39–63.

Kristensen, Mette, Marlene Jensen, Jane Kudsk, Marianne Henriksen, and Christian Mølgaard. 2005. "Short-Term Effects on Bone Turnover of Replacing Milk with Cola Beverages: A 10-Day Interventional Study in Young Men." *Osteoporosis International* 16 (12):1803–8.

Kuklys, Wiebke. 2005. *Amartya Sen's Capability Approach: Theoretical Insights and Empirical Applications*. Berlin: Springer.

Kusek, Jody Zall, and Ray C. Rist. 2004. *Ten Steps to a Results-Based Monitoring and Evaluation System: A Handbook for Development Practitioners*. Washington, DC: World Bank.

Kynch, Jocelyn, and Amartya Sen. 1983. "Indian Women: Well-Being and Survival." *Cambridge Journal of Economics* 7 (3/4):363–80.

Larmore, Charles. 2001. "A Critique of Philip Pettit's Republicanism." *Philosophical Issues* 11 (1):229–43.

Latour, Bruno. 1987. *Science in Action: How to Follow Scientists and Engineers Through Society*. Cambridge, MA: Harvard University Press.

Lelli, Laila. 2001. "Factor Analysis vs. Fuzzy Sets Theory: Assessing the Influence of Different Techniques on Sen's Functionings Approach." *KU Leuven Center for Economic Studies Discussion Paper Series*. Leuven: Katholieke Universiteit Leuven.

Lengwiler, Martin. 2008. "Participatory Approaches in Science and Technology Historical Origins and Current Practices in Critical Perspective." *Science, Technology & Human Values* 33 (2):186–200.

Lessmann, Ortrud. 2011. "Sustainability as a Challenge to the Capability Approach." In *Sustainable Development: Capabilities, Needs, and Well-Being*, edited by F. Rauschmayer, I. Omann, and J. Frühmann, 43–61. London: Routledge.

Lessmann, Ortrud, and Felix Rauschmayer. 2013. "Re-Conceptualizing Sustainable Development on the Basis of the Capability Approach: A Model and Its Difficulties." *Journal of Human Development and Capabilities* 14 (1):95–114.

Letts, Christine W., William Ryan, and Allen Grossman. 1997. "Virtuous Capital: What Foundations Can Learn from Venture Capitalists." *Harvard Business Review* 75:36–50.

List, Christian. 2006. "Republican Freedom and the Rule of Law." *Politics, Philosophy & Economics* 5 (2):201–20.

Lloyd-Sherlock, Peter. 2015. "Leave No One behind? Not If You're over 70." *Post2015.Org—What Comes After the MDGs?* (blog). http://post2015.org/2015/07/28/leave-no-one-behind-not-if-youre-over-70/.

Longino, Helen. 1983. "Beyond 'Bad Science': Skeptical Reflections on the Value-Freedom of Scientific Inquiry." *Science, Technology, & Human Values* 8 (1):7–17.

———. 1990. *Science as Social Knowledge: Values and Objectivity in Scientific Inquiry*. Princeton, NJ: Princeton University Press.

Lovett, Frank. 2001. "Domination: A Preliminary Analysis." *Monist* 84 (1):98–112.

———. 2009. "Domination and Distributive Justice." *Journal of Politics* 71 (3):817–30.

———. 2010. *A General Theory of Domination and Justice*. Oxford: Oxford University Press.

———. 2012. "What Counts as Arbitrary Power?" *Journal of Political Power* 5 (1):137–52. https://doi.org/10.1080/2158379X.2012.660026.

———. 2014. "Republicanism (Stanford Encyclopedia of Philosophy)." In *Stanford Encyclopedia of Philosophy*. http://plato.stanford.edu/entries/republicanism/.

Lovett, Frank, and Philip Pettit. 2009. "Neorepublicanism: A Normative and Institutional Research Program." *Political Science* 12 (1):11.

MacCallum, Gerald C. 1967. "Negative and Positive Freedom." *Philosophical Review* 76 (3):312–34.

Macfarlane, Bruce, and Ming Cheng. 2008. "Communism, Universalism and Disinterestedness: Re-Examining Contemporary Support among Academics for Merton's Scientific Norms." *Journal of Academic Ethics* 6 (1):67–78.

Malik, Vasanti S., Barry M. Popkin, George A. Bray, Jean-Pierre Després, and Frank B. Hu. 2010. "Sugar-Sweetened Beverages, Obesity, Type 2 Diabetes Mellitus, and Cardiovascular Disease Risk." *Circulation* 121 (11):1356–64.

Maynor, John. 2003. *Republicanism in the Modern World*. Cambridge: Polity.

———. 2006. "Modern Republican Democratic Contestation: A Model of Deliberative Democracy." In *Republicanism in Theory and Practice*, edited by Iseult Honohan and Jeremy Jennings, 125–39. London: Routledge.

McGoey, Linsey. 2012. "Philanthrocapitalism and Its Critics." *Poetics, Cultures of Circulation*, 40 (2):185–99.

McMahon, Christopher. 2005. "The Indeterminacy of Republican Policy." *Philosophy & Public Affairs* 33 (1):67–93.

Merton, Robert K. 1973. "The Normative Structure of Science." In *The Sociology of Science: Theoretical and Empirical Investigations*, edited by Norman W. Storer, 267–78. Chicago: University of Chicago Press.

Mulkay, Michael. 1979. "Knowledge and Utility: Implications for the Sociology of Knowledge." *Social Studies of Science* 9 (1):63–80.

Narayan, Deepa, Robert Chambers, Meera K. Shah, and Patti Petesch. 2000. *Voices of the Poor, Volume II: Crying Out for Change*. New York: World Bank.
Narayan, Deepa, Raj Patel, Kai Schafft, Anne Rademacher, and Sarah Koch-Schulte. 1999. *Voices of the Poor, Volume I: Can Anyone Hear Us?* Washington, DC: World Bank.
Narayan, Deepa, and Patti Petesch. 2002. *Voices of the Poor, Volume III: From Many Lands*. New York: World Bank.
Narayan-Parker, Deepa. 2002. *Empowerment and Poverty Reduction: A Sourcebook*. Washington, DC: World Bank.
———. 2005. *Measuring Empowerment: Cross-Disciplinary Perspectives*. Washington, DC: World Bank.
Nussbaum, Martha. 1990. "Aristotelian Social Democracy." In *Liberalism and the Good*, edited by R. Bruce Douglas, Gerald M. Mara, and Henry S. Richardson, 203–252. New York: Routledge.
———. 1992. "Human Functioning and Social Justice in Defense of Aristotelian Essentialism." *Political Theory* 20 (2):202–46.
———. 1995. "Aristotle on Human Nature and the Foundation of Ethics." In *World, Mind and Ethics: Essays on the Ethical Philosophy of Bernard Williams*, edited by J.E.J. Altham and Ross Harrison, 86–131. Cambridge: Cambridge University Press.
———. 2000. *Women and Human Development: The Capabilities Approach*. Cambridge: Cambridge University Press.
———. 2003. "Capabilities as Fundamental Entitlements: Sen and Social Justice." *Feminist Economics* 9 (2–3):33–59.
———. 2006. *Frontiers of Justice*. Cambridge, MA: Belknap Press of Harvard University Press.
———. 2011a. "Capabilities, Entitlements, Rights: Supplementation and Critique." *Journal of Human Development and Capabilities* 12 (1):23–37.
———. 2011b. *Creating Capabilities: The Human Development Approach*. Cambridge, MA: Belknap Press of Harvard University Press.
OECD. 1996. *Shaping the 21st Century: The Contribution of Development Co-Operation*. Paris: OECD.
———. 2005. *Paris Declaration on Aid Effectiveness*. Paris: OECD.
———. 2008. *Accra Agenda for Action*. Paris: OECD.
———. 2011. *Busan Partnership Agreement*. Paris: OECD.
Osmani, Siddiqur Rahman. 2005. "Poverty and Human Rights: Building on the Capability Approach." *Journal of Human Development* 6 (2):205–19.
Pettit, Philip. 1997. *Republicanism: A Theory of Freedom and Government*. Oxford: Oxford University Press.
———. 1999. "Republican Freedom and Contestatory Democratization." In *Democracy's Value*, edited by Ian Shapiro and Casiano Hacker-Cordon, 163–90. Cambridge: Cambridge University Pres.
———. 2004. "The Common Good." In *Justice and Democracy: Essays for Brian Barry*, edited by Keith Dowding, Robert E. Goodin, and Carole Pateman. Cambridge: Cambridge University Press.
———. 2006. "The Determinacy of Republican Policy: A Reply to McMahon." *Philosophy & Public Affairs* 34 (3):275–83.
———. 2012. *On the People's Terms: A Republican Theory and Model of Democracy*. Cambridge: Cambridge University Press.

———. 2016. "A Brief History of Liberty—and Its Lessons." *Journal of Human Development and Capabilities*, January, 1–17.

Phelps, Teresa Godwin. 2006. "Narrative Capability: Telling Stories in the Search for Justice." In *Transforming Unjust Structures: The Capability Approach*, edited by Severine Deneulin, Mathias Nebel, and Nicholas Sagovsky, 105–20. Dordrecht: Springer.

Pogge, Thomas, and Mitu Sengupta. 2015. "The Sustainable Development Goals (SDGs) as Drafted: Nice Idea, Poor Execution." *Washington International Law Journal* 24 (3):571–87.

Pressman, Steven, and Gale Summerfield. 2002. "Sen and Capabilities." *Review of Political Economy* 14 (4):429–34.

Qizilbash, Mozaffar. 1996. "Capabilities, Well-Being and Human Development: A Survey." *Journal of Development Studies* 33 (2):143–62.

———. 1998. "Poverty, Concept and Measurement." *Research Report Series*. Islamabad: Sustainable Development Policy Institute.

———. 2011. "Sugden's Critique of Sen's Capability Approach and the Dangers of Libertarian Paternalism." *International Review of Economics* 58 (1): 21–42.

———. 2012. "The Capability Approach: Its Interpretation and 'Limitations.'" In *The Capability Approach: Development Practice and Public Policy in the Asia-Pacific Region*, edited by Francesca Panzironi and Katharine Gelber, 9–22. London: Routledge.

Rauschmayer, Felix, and Ortrud Lessmann. 2011. "Assets and Drawbacks of the CA as a Foundation for Sustainability Economics." *Ecological Economics* 70 (11):1835–36.

Rauschmayer, Felix, Ines Omann, and Johannes Frühmann. 2012. *Sustainable Development: Capabilities, Needs, and Well-Being*. London: Routledge.

Rawls, John. 1999. *A Theory of Justice*. Revised Edition. Cambridge, MA: Belknap Press of Harvard University Press.

Robeyns, Ingrid. 2003. "Sen's Capability Approach and Gender Inequality: Selecting Relevant Capabilities." *Feminist Economics* 9 (2–3):61–92.

———. 2005. "The Capability Approach: A Theoretical Survey." *Journal of Human Development* 6 (1):93–117.

———. 2006. "The Capability Approach in Practice." *Journal of Political Philosophy* 14 (3):351–76.

———. 2008. "Ideal Theory in Theory and Practice." *Social Theory and Practice* 34 (3):341–62.

———. 2011. "The Capability Approach." In *Stanford Encyclopedia of Philosophy*, edited by Edward N. Zalta. http://plato.stanford.edu/entries/capability-approach/.

———. 2012. "Are Transcendental Theories of Justice Redundant?" *Journal of Economic Methodology* 19 (2):159–63.

———. 2016. "Capabilitarianism." *Journal of Human Development and Capabilities* 17 (3):397–414.

———. 2017. *Wellbeing, Freedom and Social Justice: The Capability Approach Re-Examined*. Cambridge, UK: Open Book Publishers.

Rodrigue, Jean-Paul, and Claude Comtois. 2013. "Transportation and Energy." In *The Geography of Transport Systems*, edited by Jean-Paul Rodrigue, Claude Comtois, and Brian Slack. New York: Routledge.

Sadler, Troy D. 2004. "Informal Reasoning Regarding Socioscientific Issues: A Critical Review of Research." *Journal of Research in Science Teaching* 41 (5):513–36.

Seely, Bruce E. 1996. "State Engineers as Policymakers: Apolitical Experts in a Federalist System." In *Civil Engineering History: Engineers Make History*, edited by Jerry R. Rogers, Donald Kennon, Robert T. Jaske, and Francis E. Griggs, 123–35. New York: American Society of Civil Engineers.

Sen, Amartya. 1974. "Informational Bases of Alternative Welfare Approaches: Aggregation and Income Distribution." *Journal of Public Economics* 3 (4):387–403.

———. 1979a. "Equality of What?" In *The Tanner Lectures on Human Values*, edited by S. McMurrin, 196–220. Salt Lake City: University of Utah Press.

———. 1979b. "Issues in the Measurement of Poverty." *Scandinavian Journal of Economics* 81 (2):285–307.

———. 1979c. "Utilitarianism and Welfarism." *Journal of Philosophy* 76 (9):463–89.

———. 1979d. "Personal Utilities and Public Judgements: Or What's Wrong with Welfare Economics." *Economic Journal* 89 (355):537–58.

———. 1980. "Famines." *World Development* 8 (9):613–21.

———. 1985a. *Commodities and Capabilities*. Oxford: Oxford University Press.

———. 1985b. "Well-Being, Agency and Freedom: The Dewey Lectures 1984." *Journal of Philosophy* 82 (4):169–221.

———. 1988. "Freedom of Choice: Concept and Content." *European Economic Review* 32 (2–3):269–94.

———. 1989. "Development as Capability Expansion." *Journal of Development Planning* 19:41–58.

———. 1997a. "Editorial: Human Capital and Human Capability." *World Development* 25 (12):1959–61.

———. 1997b. "Maximization and the Act of Choice." *Econometrica* 65 (4):745–79.

———. 1999a. "Democracy as a Universal Value." *Journal of Democracy* 10 (3):3–17.

———. 1999b. *Development as Freedom*. New York: Knopf.

———. 2001. "Democracy and Social Justice." In *Democracy, Market Economics, and Development: An Asian Perspective*, edited by Farrukh Iqbal and Jong-Il You, 7–24. Washington, DC: World Bank.

———. 2002. *Rationality and Freedom*. Cambridge, MA: Harvard University Press.

———. 2005. "Human Rights and Capabilities." *Journal of Human Development* 6 (2):151–66.

———. 2006. "What Do We Want from a Theory of Justice?" *Journal of Philosophy* 103 (5):215–38.

———. 2009. *The Idea of Justice*. Cambridge, MA: Belknap Press of Harvard University Press.

Sen, Amartya, and Thomas Scanlon. 2004. "What's the Point of Democracy." *American Academy of Arts and Sciences Bulletin* 57 (3):9–11.

Sen, Bharati. 2005. "Indigenous Knowledge for Development: Bringing Research and Practice Together." *International Information & Library Review* 37 (4):375–82.

Sengupta, Arjun. 2002. "On the Theory and Practice of the Right to Development." *Human Rights Quarterly* 24 (4):837–89.

Sengupta, Mitu. 2016. "The Sustainable Development Goals: An Assessment of Ambition." *E-International Relations*, January 18, 2016. www.e-ir.info/2016/01/18/the-sustainable-development-goals-an-assessment-of-ambition/.

Sillitoe, Paul. 1998. "The Development of Indigenous Knowledge: A New Applied Anthropology." *Current Anthropology* 39 (2):223–52.

———. 2004. "Interdisciplinary Experiences: Working with Indigenous Knowledge in Development." *Interdisciplinary Science Reviews* 29 (1):6–23.

Skinner, Quentin. 1998. *Liberty before Liberalism*. Cambridge: Cambridge University Press.

Slottje, Daniel J. 1991. "Measuring the Quality of Life across Countries." *The Review of Economics and Statistics* 73 (4):684–93.

Smith, Andrew F. 2014. "Political Deliberation and the Challenge of Bounded Rationality." *Politics, Philosophy & Economics* 13 (3):269–91.

Steiner, Hillel. 1994. *An Essay on Rights*. Oxford: Blackwell.

Stemplowska, Zofia. 2008. "What's Ideal About Ideal Theory?" *Social Theory and Practice* 34 (3):319–40.

Stewart, Frances. 2015. "The Sustainable Development Goals: A Comment." *Journal of Global Ethics* 11 (3):288–93.

Stiglitz, Joseph E., Amartya Sen, and Jean-Paul Fitoussi. 2010. *Report by the Commission on the Measurement of Economic Performance and Social Progress*. Paris: Commission on the Measurement of Economic Performance and Social Progress.

Streeten, Paul. 1994. "Human Development: Means and Ends." *American Economic Review* 84 (2):232–7.

Sugden, Robert. 2006. "What We Desire, What We Have Reason to Desire, Whatever We Might Desire: Mill and Sen on the Value of Opportunity." *Utilitas* 18 (1):33.

———. 2008. "Capability, Happiness and Opportunity." In *Capabilities and Happiness*, edited by Luigino Bruni, Flavio Comim, and Maurizio Pugno, 299–322. Oxford: Oxford University Press.

Taylor, Charles. 1985. "What's Wrong with Negative Liberty." In *Philosophical Papers. Vol. 2: Philosophy and the Human Sciences*, 211–29. Cambridge: Cambridge University Press.

———. 1991. *The Malaise of Modernity*. Toronto: House of Anansi.

———. 1993. "Modernity and the Rise of the Public Sphere." *Tanner Lectures on Human Values* 14:203–60.

UN Inter-agency Group for Child Mortality Estimation. 2014. *Levels and Trends in Child Mortality: Report 2014*. New York: UNICEF.

UNESCO Institute for Statistics. "International Literacy Data 2013." Accessed November 28, 2014. www.uis.unesco.org/literacy/Pages/data-release-map-2013.aspx.

UNDP. 2015. "Human Development Report 2015." New York: United Nations Development Programme.

United Nations. 2000. "United Nations Millennium Declaration."

———. 2001. "Road Map Towards the Implementation of the United Nations Millennium Declaration (A /56/326)."

———. 2012. "The Future We Want: Outcome Document Adopted at Rio+20."

———. 2013. "Open Working Group of the General Assembly on Sustainable Development Goals (A/67/L.48/Rev.1)."

———. 2014. "Modalities for the Process of Intergovernmental Negotiations on the Post-2015 Development Agenda (A/69/L.46)."

———. 2015a. "Transforming Our World: The 2030 Agenda for Sustainable Development (A/RES/70/1)."

———. 2015b. "United Nations Millennium Development Goals."

Valentini, Laura. 2011. "A Paradigm Shift in Theorizing about Justice? A Critique of Sen." *Economics and Philosophy* 27 (3):297–315.

———. 2012. "Ideal vs. Non-Ideal Theory: A Conceptual Map." *Philosophy Compass* 7 (9):654–64.

Vallentyne, Peter. 2005. "Debate: Capabilities Versus Opportunities for Well-Being." *Journal of Political Philosophy* 13 (3):359–71.

Vandemoortele, Jan. 2012. *Advancing the Global Development Agenda Post-2015: Some Thoughts, Ideas and Practical Suggestions*. New York: UN System Task Team on the Post-2015 UN Development Agenda.

———. 2015a. "A Dispassionate Look at the Sustainable Development Goals." *Post2015.Org—What Comes After the MDGs?* (blog). http://post2015.org/2015/08/27/a-dispassionate-look-at-the-sustainable-development-goals/.

———. 2015b. "Does LNOB Really Merit so Much Attention?" *Post2015.Org—What Comes After the MDGs?* (blog). http://post2015.org/2015/07/31/does-lnob-really-merit-so-much-attention/.

———. 2015c. "From 'System 1' MDGs to 'System 2' SDGs: The Wrong Way?" *Post2015.Org—What Comes After the MDGs?* (blog). http://post2015.org/2015/05/11/from-system-1-mdgs-to-system-2-sdgs-the-wrong-way/.

Vizard, Polly. 2006. *Poverty and Human Rights: Sen's "Capability Perspective" Explored*. Oxford: Oxford University Press.

———. 2007. "Specifying and Justifying a Basic Capability Set: Should the International Human Rights Framework Be Given a More Direct Role?" *Oxford Development Studies* 35 (3):225–50.

———. 2010. "Developing and Agreeing a Capability List in the British Context: What Can Be Learnt from Social Survey Data on 'Rights'?" CASE Working Papers 142. London: London School of Economics.

Volkert, Jürgen, ed. 2005. *Armut und Reichtum an Verwirklichungschancen: Amartya Sens Capability-Konzept als Grundlage der Armuts- und Reichtumsberichterstattung*. Wiesbaden: VS Verlag für Sozialwissenschaften.

Waldmueller, Johannes M. 2015. "Agriculture, Knowledge and the 'Colonial Matrix of Power': Approaching Sustainabilities from the Global South." *Journal of Global Ethics* 11 (3):294–302.

Walker, Melanie. 2006. "Towards a Capability-based Theory of Social Justice for Education Policy-making." *Journal of Education Policy* 21 (2):163–85.

Walzer, Michael. 1981. "Philosophy and Democracy." *Political Theory* 9 (3):379–99.

———. 1983. *Spheres of Justice: A Defense of Pluralism and Equality*. New York: Basic Books.

Warner, Koko, Tamer Afifi, Walter Kälin, Scott Leckie, Beth Ferris, Susan F. Martin, and David Wrathall. 2013. *Changing Climate, Moving People: Framing Migration, Displacement and Planned Relocation*. Bonn, Germany: United Nations University Institute for Environment and Human Security.

Wartenberg, Thomas E. 1990. *The Forms of Power: From Domination to Transformation*. Philadelphia, PA: Temple University Press.
Watene, Krushil. 2013. "Nussbaum's Capability Approach and Future Generations." *Journal of Human Development and Capabilities* 14 (1):21–39.
Watene, Krushil, and Mandy Yap. 2015. "Culture and Sustainable Development: Indigenous Contributions." *Journal of Global Ethics* 11 (1):51–5.
Weintraub, Jeff, and Krishan Kumar. 1997. *Public and Private in Thought and Practice: Perspectives on a Grand Dichotomy*. Chicago: University of Chicago Press.
Wilson, Gordon. 2006. "Beyond the Technocrat? The Professional Expert in Development Practice." *Development and Change* 37 (3):501–23.
Wisor, Scott. 2012. "After the MDGs: Citizen Deliberation and the Post-2015 Development Framework." *Ethics & International Affairs* 26 (1):113–33.
Woodward, Alison E., Jean-Michel Bonvin, and Mercè Renom. 2011. "The Impact of Social Movements on Gendered Well-Being in Europe." In *Transforming Gendered Well-Being in Europe: The Impact of Social Movements*, edited by Jean-Michel Bonvin, Mercè Renom, and Alison E. Woodward, 265–272. London and New York: Routledge.
Woolgar, Steve. 1988. *Science: The Very Idea*. New York: Methuen.
World Bank. 1994. *World Bank and Participation*. Washington, DC: World Bank.
World Health Organization. 2015. "Adolescent Pregnancy." www.who.int/maternal_child_adolescent/topics/maternal/adolescent_pregnancy/en/.
Wynne, Brian. 1989. "Sheepfarming After Chernobyl: A Case Study in Communicating Scientific Information." *Environment: Science and Policy for Sustainable Development* 31 (2):10–39.
Zanden, Jan Luiten van, Joerg Baten, Marco Mira d'Ercole, Auke Rjpma, Conal Smith, and Marcel Timmer. 2014. *How Was Life? Global Well-Being Since 1820*. Paris: OECD.

Index

www.ingramcontent.com/pod-product-compliance
Ingram Content Group UK Ltd.
Pitfield, Milton Keynes, MK11 3LW, UK
UKHW021300190926
475701UK00009B/88
9780367734664